THE BIG UNLOCK

THE BIG UNLOCK

Liberate Your Creativity Through Mindful Journaling

BY LAURA L. RUBIN

New York Amsterdam/Antwerp London
Toronto Sydney/Melbourne New Delhi

An Imprint of Simon & Schuster, LLC
1230 Avenue of the Americas
New York, NY 10020

First Simon Element hardcover edition March 2026

SIMON ELEMENT is a registered trademark of Simon & Schuster, LLC

INTERIOR DESIGN BY KARLA SCHWEER

Manufactured in the United States of America

10 9 8 7 6 5 4 3 2 1

Library of Congress Control Number has been applied for.

ISBN 978-1-6680-8205-8
ISBN 978-1-6680-8207-2 (ebook)

For DSR.
Wherever you are, I think you know.

CONTENTS

INTRODUCTION

I might've been early, but I wasn't wrong. Over a decade ago, I recognized that journaling had a major PR problem. As a marketing and communications executive, part of my job was to be a futurist, to predict what people will want and need before they know it. And the tea leaves weren't looking good. Both in that role and on an interpersonal level, I was witnessing how massively dissociated our culture had become, and I knew that analog self-expression could help. But at the time, journaling was closely associated with cringe poetry, angsty teen scribblings, and overly scented bath products, despite it being a science-backed, effective, and legitimate modality for mental, emotional, and physiological well-being. I wanted to get more people to the page, but I also recognized that accomplishing this required us to shift the cultural connotations about what it means to keep a journal.

To start chipping away at the misconceptions, I created a gender-neutral brand, AllSwell Creative, influenced by my time in and on the ocean. It began with design-forward, analog products, including a series of write/draw notebooks, a deck of thoughtful prompts, packs of cheeky postcards, and more. My thinking: Make it attractive. Make it feel good. The people will come. And they did. A dedicated community coalesced around putting pen to paper. But the marketplace also quickly taught me that the process of mindful writing, which has been intuitive for me since I opened my first journal when my age was just a single digit, is intimidating to others. Scary, even. It turns out, people have some major journaling hang-ups.

Addressing this, I crafted a curriculum of guided sessions that came under the AllSwell umbrella. I made my approach enjoyable, approachable, visually inviting, and even aspirational. Less precious, more Prada. I wove peer-reviewed scientific research throughout to assuage left-brain concerns and avoid any lightweight, "hippie" connotations. Less Boulder, Colorado, more Bain consulting. All of this was carefully architected to infiltrate cultural sectors that wouldn't otherwise take journaling seriously, and to help get ink flowing.

In the early days, when I shared the concept with business-minded decision-makers, their responses often resembled bored or quizzical looks. The same people who sought out my professional opinions as a brand marketer were frequently dismissive, occasionally even snarky. (At one point, a contact took me out for coffee to apologize for having ridiculed my business behind my back to our mutual professional colleagues.) For the most part, this pushback fueled my intent, but when I occasionally got discouraged, I reminded myself that this endeavor wasn't really about me. The practice of journaling supports others in ways that are badly, urgently needed.

Pen-to-paper is the antivenom for our digital malaise. "How are you?" seems like a basic question, but it's become increasingly difficult to answer in the age of distraction. We're in a constant state of react-and-respond from the first moment we glance at the brilliant little phones in our hands. Our brains navigate wave after wave of data specifically tailored to our interests, concerns, and tastes, with cues cleverly designed to engage us, hook us, sell to us.[1]

We sleep with our phones under our pillows, checking devices before we've had coffee, let alone pee.[2] (Uncivilized, but statistically true.) We're losing vital opportunities to be creative, ceding them to artificial intelligence and pervasive busyness, yet we've never been hungrier for meaning.

Many of us are on a steady digital diet of psychological junk food, stuffing it in by the fistful and wondering why we feel unnourished. To state the obvious, this is not healthy.

Amidst these challenges, it has become uniquely difficult to know how we actually feel, what we derive meaning from, and even who we are. While the answers to these questions will differ from individual to individual, they don't come from external sources. Mindful journaling helps us thread our way through these tempestuous times, unlocking access to what is true and real, what our values and visions are. Pen in hand, a sense of purpose comes into view.

And the zeitgeist has started to catch up. Today nobody glazes over when I tell them what I do for a living. They're intrigued, curious, engaged, sometimes verging on needy. Like a dermatologist at a cocktail party being asked to look at a mole, people pull me aside to share their concerns and desires to journal, peppering me with questions. Why? Wave after wave of burnout. We are beyond burnt; our culture is outright crispy.

I've now led hundreds of guided journaling sessions for thousands of people, including some unlikely groups of staunch capitalists and technologists. I've collected the learnings, anecdotes, and best practices and poured them into these pages. Like a surfer builds out their quiver of boards for different conditions, *The Big Unlock* stocks your journaling tool kit with a broad range of ways to reveal and encourage your creativity. You can access them wherever, whenever you want them. No appointment or preauthorization required.

We need solutions for who we are now to help shape who we will become, both as individuals and as a collective. Once we quiet the noise yanking our attention around like a rag doll, our discernment sharpens, and information has the chance to reveal itself on the page. By liberating your creativity, the machete in your pencil materializes. It can clear a path through digital debris, freeing up mindshare and revealing a sane, inspiring, and bountiful way forward. Welcome to the mindful writing revolution.

How to use this book

This is intentionally not a workbook. You won't find lines to fill in after each prompt because that sets up limitations, and we are in the business of picking locks between you and your creative process, not adding them. Take up as much (or as little) space to respond to these prompts as you need.

To accompany your experience of exploring *The Big Unlock*, choose a notebook. Lined or unlined, small enough to fit in a breast pocket or big enough to let your thoughts roam around on the page. Marbled composition book or a leather-bound diary, pen or pencil, whatever materials feel right, those are the right ones for you.

If you don't have your notebook at hand but the impulse to journal strikes, you can use the blank "Notes" pages at the end of the book. Got your back.

You don't need to move through this book cover to cover. It's okay to skip around. I designed it so that each chapter can stand on its own, though the four parts build on the one/s prior, as we wade into deeper waters together.

Not all chapters may seem like they pertain to you. Feel free to cherry-pick, but let yourself be curious. Even if a theme doesn't seem specifically suited to your pain points (e.g., grieving) or psychographic (such as masculine self-expression), the chapter may well meet needs you didn't even realize you had.

So dog-ear, underline, annotate. But, most of all, enjoy.

PART I

Living Unlocked:

The Groundwork for Your Mindful Writing Practice

Herein lie foundational steps and tactics, plus answers to more than a decade's worth of FAQs. This section introduces you to the AllSwell approach to journaling, specifically, and my perspective on creativity, more generally. We're planting seeds in fertile soil, and watering them.

If you've never journaled before, then welcome. This is a solid place to start. And if you're already an avid journaler, these chapters can help you expand and explore your practice while significantly increasing its upsides.

1

The Guru Is You:

NO, REALLY

Wouldn't it be great if I had all the answers for you? Well, I don't. That's not me and it's certainly not this book. It's better.

Through the approach to intentional journaling that's laid out over the course of these chapters, you will discover and hone a series of elegant, effective keys that help unlock your unique creative potential. Through them, you'll gain access to agency, ignite innovation, reveal clarity, and craft an authentic, inspired life. What this process offers is worlds better than borrowed slogans or blanket pronouncements. Your intelligence, imagination, and intuition are invited to come out and play on the page. There will be loads of support from me along the way, but the wisdom in those keys isn't mine. It's yours.

Never in human history have we had such unfettered access to external advice, and with that comes a lot of false idols and empty claims.[1] Everywhere we look or listen, a fire hose of information instructs us how to become optimized versions of ourselves, and not all of it is properly vetted or applicable. The result can be an expensive, confusing, or even dangerous cacophony of contradicting instruction.

"Is tart cherry juice what I've been missing?"

"Do I need to do a heavy metal detox?"

"Intermittent fasting will change my life."

"Scratch that. Cold plunging will change my life."

"Veganism will save us all."

"Eat more protein. Lift more weights."

"Do I need a shamanic colonic?"

"Clearly my problem is that I'm not manifesting correctly."

It's advice overwhelm. Foundationally, the voice you're looking for—the one with the bespoke, paradigm-changing wisdom that is right and real for you—is likely your own. And journaling is an effective way to connect with it via a clear, direct channel. There's no intermediary on the page. Free-write for long enough, and you'll discover internally generated insights. That's right: *The guru is you.*

Even when I lead an AllSwell workshop, I see my role as setting the scene, providing context, offering up valuable prompts, and then getting out of the way. I'm not telling anyone what to write. Yes, I shepherd participants through the process, but the words (and sometimes images) they put on the page are their own. What shows up ranges from thoughtfully insightful to radically life altering.

We're all subject to various sources of programming, which impacts our identity. Gender, race, religion, financial strata, birth order, education, size of family, even hair color or what street you live on. Cumulatively, this programming becomes a lot of subtle (or not so subtle) expectations for an individual to wade through. Some of it can be well-intentioned, such as familial belief systems. "Marry a doctor," said your great-aunt because she thought that resulted in financial security, a way to keep you safe. Misguided but well-meaning. Regardless of intent or accuracy, it's still not intrinsic. It's easy to mistake programming for identity, but it's not necessarily who you are and may be holding you back. Via mindful journaling, we'll write our way out of this hall of mirrors to clarity.

Sloughing off what doesn't serve and landing quietly in your own knowing takes practice. It certainly did for me. Whether you're nodding in agreement or not quite sure what I'm talking about, here's a journaling prompt to help you cultivate your inner acuity. Take it for a spin.

PROMPT: When was a time you trusted your own judgment and it served you well? Maybe your community didn't agree, the prevailing norm would have instructed otherwise, or the decision was simply out of character for you. The instance can be something as simple as what you ordered for lunch, or a pivotal, personal sea change like leaving a business or a relationship. Reflect and write.

A half page will do as a starting point. After all, we're just getting acquainted.

If you find this prompt challenging, don't strain yourself. Skip this exercise for now, and circle back any time you're keen. Either way, let's keep going.

As both a journalist and occasional subject, I flip-flop between being an interviewer and an interviewee. A standard question I've been asked repeatedly is some variation of this: "What's the best piece of advice you've ever received?" My go-to answer is, "Trust your gut." Value your own counsel. Not instead of remaining curious and benefiting from credible resources. That, too. I'm a data nerd, always on the lookout for new sources of insights, but I've had to learn to acknowledge and appreciate my most personal intelligence, and the page is where I find it.

We're going to turn that business-as-usual interview question upside down. On its head it can be pretty illuminating.

PROMPT: What's the best piece of advice you've given someone else? Who did you give it to, and how did you come to have this wisdom? How did you earn this valuable piece of awareness? Let's give this a whole page, or more.

As I'm sure you noticed, neither of these prompts are about reiterating third-party insights. Because thoughtful advice and mentoring are great tools, but ultimately the choices we make, and the identity we claim as our own, are up to us.

Journaling is how I've made every major life decision. Abandon the corporate ladder and start my own entrepreneurial venture. Check. Pivot my business to an entirely new industry despite signs to the contrary. Yup. When to move across the country (and back). Correct and correct again. When to not marry that wonderful guy.

Hard but true. Abandon my efforts to conceive a child and instead channel that generative energy elsewhere. Gulp. Sigh. Yes. I also talked these choices over with trusted sources, but the decisions were my own. They came from a place deep within me, and I journaled my way to that resource. The result has been a life that's a beautiful experiment, one that is unique, dynamic, full, and satisfying more days than not.

Shushing the external programming and clearing a path to yourself—your truths and interests—is one of the considerable gifts that coming to the page delivers. It turns down the volume on what's dissonant, helping us discern what's junk versus what's endemic to the version you are today and the one you'd like to become tomorrow. Guides and interpreters aside, eventually it's going to be your decisions that build your life. Make it a life that you love, and write your way there.

2

Inherent Creativity:

NOT JUST FOR WRITERS AND ARTISTS

"But I'm not creative" is one of the common concerns I hear from those questioning their ability to journal. Somewhere along the way, they may have been told they aren't artistic, don't have taste, are bad at writing, etc. They started to believe they don't have the ability to make stuff.

But here's a big and real truth. Each human on this planet is a creative being. Accountants, plumbers, COOs and CEOs, car mechanics, oncologists, bus drivers, math teachers, your next-door neighbor. We all have a rich wellspring of creativity within that we access every day. Daydreams are creativity at work. So is problem-solving in any capacity. Every time you make a decision, choosing from among multiple options, you are not just employing logic; you're also imagining outcomes. Yup, that's creativity again. When you are firing up your brain to conjure something from nothing (which we do countless times a day), that requires vision. It might not show up on a canvas, but you are frequently employed in the act of creation.

Over and over, I've witnessed innovative interpretations of a writing prompt emerge from some of the most (seemingly) surprising characters. They didn't realize they were being inventive; more likely, they were concerned that they hadn't followed the rules. In a tent full of data analysts, a workshop participant shared apologetically that writing wasn't really for him, so he'd drawn all of his answers. I beamed. *Hell, yeah* he did. This individual had just spent ninety minutes taking writing cues and translating them into drawing exercises, making them utterly his own. He hadn't *misinterpreted* the exercises. He'd *reinterpreted* them.

Rules and limitations can be a means of exploration—something for us to react to, yielding new expressions. But not always. (The constraints of iambic pentameter aren't for everyone, including me.) Part of the AllSwell approach is making it okay for you to interpret the exercises and prompts you find on these pages, however you see fit. I'm not here to tell you that you've done it badly or incorrectly. There is no "bad"; there is just "do." Similarly, you don't need to be a good writer to excel at journaling. There's no third-party reader, and you receive the mental, emotional, and physiological benefits regardless of your grammar, spelling, or even the quality of your handwriting. With that in mind, let's explore a prompt.

PROMPT: When was a time that you didn't follow the rules . . . and the outcome was beneficial? Where were you? Whose rules were they (maybe they were self-imposed)? What was the result, and how did it feel? Who did it help out? What did you learn?

Deviating from norms takes courage and vision. What we often realize too little (or what can feel like too late) is that our lives are a creative act. Each day, we are writing scripts for ourselves, making choices and interpreting what we think we should do, weighing it against what we can do, and perhaps even what we believe we were meant to do.

Despite our innate creative abilities, practice helps. That's where the page meets you. You are safe between the front and back covers of your notebook, so go ahead and let things get messy (I'm talking to you, perfectionists). Invite impulses of exploration into a no-risk environment and see what arises. Channel the energy of a kiddo in kindergarten art class. It probably won't turn you into Rembrandt, but you're smart enough to know that's not the point. Ingenuity isn't relegated to the world of high art—or, for that matter, even artists—and you certainly don't need to "suffer for your art" (my least favorite trope) to have an imagination and make good use of it.

When you are in consistent dialogue with your creative energies via journaling, they're probably going to start showing up in other parts of your world, too. You might become a better manager, a more inventive and curious parent, emboldened to try out something new that interests you even if it doesn't seem logical or productive. Wherever that good stuff starts to appear, it will enrich your life. I'd bet all my pencils on it.

3

Free-Range Journaling:

DON'T FENCE ME IN

Part of what I find so ridiculous about the usual journaling gestalt is how precious it is. As if to journal effectively, you must be wrapped in a chenille blanket, sipping lavender tea at sunrise, writing about how your high school crush broke your heart and you will absolutely never, ever recover. No. That ain't it, folks. And not just because I loathe chenille and lavender gives me hives.

Let's not be too la-di-da about it. When I started AllSwell, it was with the intention of upending preconceptions about keeping a journal. The act of writing may be sacred to me, but a journal can be used and abused. Espresso stains, beer-bottle labels stuck to the covers, pages warped by saltwater stains—all mean she's been some places and seen some things. A full notebook that bears the marks of the world is one sexy sight.

If you want a free-range life, a solid way to start is with your journal. Don't be a good little chicken in the coop. Go rogue—and bring a pen.

- Write anywhere, everywhere. In a crowd, on a bus, at a football game, in the mountains, on the subway, at a concert.

- Going on a trip (literal or otherwise)? Take a notebook and pen along, and it becomes a journey.

- This is meant to be messy. Feel free to rip, tear, burn, flush, cut, and lacerate those pages. Your journal doesn't mind one bit.

Once you toss limiting expectations about what it means to journal, your notebook yields so many more ways to be a potent tool, including an analog, pen-to-paper exercise I call "Repeat After Me."

PROMPT: Thematic language has immense power. What do you want to cultivate? What is your one word now? (Examples: limitless, flexible, emboldened, free, calm, delight, pleasure, play.)

Write your word down multiple times in your notebook with some space to breathe around each one. You're claiming this mantra via repetition. I like ALL CAPS for clarity and commitment.

Don't keep the sentiment confined between covers. Next, cut or rip the words out individually, then tape and place them in multiple spots where you'll see them every day. Maybe in your wallet, on the inside of the medicine cabinet, or where you keep your coffee beans. More digitally inclined? Write the word out in daily reminders that pop up in your calendar at unusual times. You're interrupting the usual mental loops by repeatedly bringing your attention back to this word.

If you stop noticing your wise scraps, move them to new spots so you continue to see them multiple times a day. All of this is in service of infusing your theme into your awareness, letting the concept percolate into your behavior.

It's more than okay to make a mess out of your notebook. It's a place you can practice giving yourself the gift of permission to be wildly, uniquely imperfect. Case in point, I sat having an afternoon coffee with an accomplished woman who shared that she felt the act of journaling was so important that it deserved elegant cursive, and so she needed to meet this challenge with her very best, creating attractive pages worthy of posterity. That's a lot of unnecessary pressure. It's not going in a frame. Distracted by how her handwriting looked, she had a hard time putting pen to paper regularly or freely.

I gently pointed out that the only person keeping score here was her, and she was being pretty mean about it. As she sighed in recognition, I shared that, in all my nerdy research, at no point have I come across a study that cites quality of handwriting as a determining factor for reaping the benefits of journaling. And since rereading your notebooks is optional, these pages may never even be seen again. Keeping it neat and tidy doesn't help us here. Being uninhibited does.

Similarly, don't relegate your mindful writing to picturesque, unhurried settings. Idealizing it cheats you out of access. Instead, fit journaling in where and when you can. My prescription for perfectionism is this: Rather than trying to fill up a notebook page by page with exquisitely executed ink, *empty it.* After each session, rip out your entry, crumple it up, and toss it away. Lower the bar of expectation and get unfussy. Be meticulous in other settings—it only clogs up the creative arteries here. By all means, if you're floating around the Balearic Islands by boat, bust out your notebook and take in your whereabouts. Soak it up. But don't wait for ideal, social media–friendly scenarios in order to crack a notebook, because it's through repetition that the greatest, cumulative benefits are accessed.[1] Here and now will do. Good is plenty good enough.

4

An On-Ramp:

MICRODOSE YOUR JOURNALING

By now, I've heard pretty much any and every reason a person could conjure for why journaling is elusive. But whatever the lock is, we can pick it. It's just a matter of identifying the ways that best fit your needs and daily rhythms.

Let's start with the pervasive time famine. "I'm too busy. I don't have time to journal." Look, I get it. As a hardworking entrepreneur, journalist, and founder, I spin a lot of plates. It's also important to me to reliably show up as a daughter, friend, sister, partner, aunt, godmother, dog mom, and mentor. Add to that life maintenance and the digital-communications vortex, and there isn't a boatload of disposable time left over. But boatloads or even truckloads of time aren't required to reap the benefits of a pen-to-paper practice.

You don't need to write a novel every day. Ease on in with what I call 4 x 4 x 4. This approach to journaling is ideal for those who don't know where to begin or say they cannot spare the time to do any mindful writing.

How 4 x 4 x 4 works:

- Journal for four minutes a day.
- Try to do it four days a week.
- Stick with it for four consecutive weeks.

Consider this a "microdose" method. You'll get used to sitting down and writing, and cumulatively you'll feel the results, all while developing journaling muscle memory via a habitual practice.

Don't take my word for it. A member of the AllSwell community shared her experience: "This method was helpful in creating a journaling routine that I can actually stick to . . . the more of an overthinker you are, the more you need to journal for your own sanity. And 4 x 4 x 4 is great for getting a routine going so that you can get a better feeling as to how much you need to/would like to journal."[1]

4 x 4 x 4 becomes a jumping-off point, helping you wade into the mindful writing. No awkward belly flops into the deep end here. Set the bar at a place that feels attainable, and it will spark positive associations. Instead of making a bigger or more frequent commit-

ment, which might not be realistic, you'll enjoy a welcome shot of dopamine from the sense of accomplishment.[2] You'll be more likely to stick with it, and the cumulative effects are where the bigger benefits are stashed.

Even the busiest people I advise can find four minutes a few times a week. For example, I met a woman, let's call her Linda, in a multisession series I led in Los Angeles.[3] She was a solo parent of four kiddos, navigating a divorce while making a living as an artist. Much respect for this lady. Linda joined our workshops because she badly wanted to journal. But she was too time poor (and distracted) to implement a pen-to-paper practice at home. The only space this hardworking momma found to journal was after the last of the morning school drops. She pulled over by the side of the road, fished a notebook and pen out of her bag, leaned against the steering wheel, and wrote for four minutes. When C-suite executives tell me they're far too busy, I cite this example. If Linda can do it, so can we.

And by taking control of sixteen minutes of your week, setting that time aside for your creativity and physiological well-being, you're establishing a powerful precedent. We often have more autonomy than we realize, particularly when we step away from the nonstop digital treadmill. You're starting at 4 x 4 x 4, but chances are, it's not where you'll end up.

Another AllSwell community member shared, "One thing that has really helped me in my practice is just keeping up the 4 x 4. I've managed to maintain it for forty-one weeks now. For me, it made sense to just keep going outside the 'trial' period. It's a good nudge to sit down with pen and book and catch up at some point in the day, to breathe a bit of space into place."[4] His interpretation became 4 x 4 x *41*—and beyond. Bravo to that.

Which illustrates, there's no wrong combo here. Maybe you'll choose to explore what 6 x 6 x 6 feels like.

Or 5 x 3 x 5.

Or 7 x 4 x 4.

Or 9 x 3 x 8.

Adapt the ritual and make it your own. Whatever amount of time you pick, I strongly recommend trying to write for the entire increment. It gives you the opportunity to journal your way past the clutter of daily gripes and connect with what's really going on under the hood. Once you've written away the surface layer of "grime," what's revealed is information that's often been waiting for a space to emerge. Intuitive hits, shimmering desires, worthy questions, the start of an idea, an image coming into focus.

If the tank starts to run dry and you still have a few minutes remaining, try writing about why you think you've run out of things to say. It's a rich vein to tap. Similarly, if you're feeling annoyed and think that journaling is a waste of your precious time, then write about your relationship to time—how you want to use it, rather than be subject to it. (After all, time is a rather arbitrary human construct.[5] How's that for a trippy concept to unpack on the page?) Essentially, write into any resistance. It might just be the inflection point you need on that given day.

While you're at it, bear in mind that 4 x 4 x 4 isn't intended to have the rigor of intermittent fasting. It's simply a framework. If you drift away from the practice, you don't have to start all over. You didn't fail journaling. All of this is an experiment, an exploration. Just bring your attention back to the page and keep going.

Once you've built up mindful writing muscles, you can experiment with time and frequency. On a slow, unprogrammed Sunday morning I might write for thirty minutes. That's not happening on a commitment-heavy Tuesday, when I might be able to sneak in only four minutes of notebook time when I'm powering down at the end of the day.

Whatever commitment you set for yourself, if you feel it isn't quite enough for a particular session, just roll right past the timer and stay in your flow state. Write until you feel complete. Write yourself clean. Then close your notebook, and go on with your day, buoyed with the knowledge that you chose to show up for yourself on the page.

5

By Any Means Necessary:

LESS DOGMA, MORE FLEXIBILITY

I'm a big proponent of longhand, but I'm not a journaling snob. Whatever you use to get the job done, it's better than not doing it. Store stray thoughts in your Notes app, emote in a Google doc, break out a Sharpie, let your thumbs explore a journaling app—it all gets you headed in the right general direction. I'll even give voice memos a nod if that's all you can muster. My general approach to creative self-expression is "better out than in," and whichever paths you use to do that have intrinsic value.

I was surprised to learn that a client of mine cited grammar software as a platform he used to organize his erratic thoughts while journaling electronically about a difficult personal topic. It worked for him as part of his creative process, going from mental chaos to clarity. So as much as I want all of us to diminish our screen time and reduce A.I. interaction, I'm not going to be prissy and dismiss a software program when my client shared that's part of how breakthroughs found him.

It should come as no surprise that pen-to-paper is my go-to, and for very good reasons. A frequent hesitation I hear about longhand journaling is, "But my hand can't keep up with the speed of my thoughts." So you have to slow things down? That sounds like a bonus to me. In addition to slowing your cerebral roll, there are certain synaptic connections made only when writing by hand.[1] Your conceptual understanding[2] and memory recall[3] both improve. (Basically, writing by hand helps you learn stuff, and then it helps you remember what you've learned.[4]) So for those of you who are efficiency minded, if you're going to take the time to journal, picking up a pen provides the biggest possible upside.

Plus, I find handwriting to be more permissive and intimate than a keyboard. Recording our thoughts and feelings on a physical page actually tends to be more private than whatever we type into a connected device. That's shareability ad infinitum.

But we don't need to get puritanical about it. Different mediums have different creative strengths, uses, and nuances. Occasionally, during one of my journaling sessions, an idea or concept starts to take shape. It arrives, tugs at my sleeve, asking for more focused attention. It doesn't want to be in Sunday driver mode; it's itching for fifth gear at the racetrack. That's when I know it's time to do what I call "the hop," jumping from notebook to keyboard.

Your journal can serve as a starting point for creative endeavors—in my case, business concerns, book and article titles, ideas, newsletter topics, etc. Longhand is an encouraging launchpad, but it may not be the best tool to fully midwife a concept. Typing is sometimes more practical when you're in a groove.

Conversely, there are some kinds of output that just do not flow for me at a keyboard, particularly when I'm naming a product (such as a mindful writing course, a retreat, etc.), making decisions (weighing pros and cons), or knocking at the door of something new (but I'm not even quite sure what it is yet). I need the flexibility and space to move words around on a page, make some bigger than others, maybe organize things in columns, give them room to morph, and let embryonic ideas take shape. I've learned to recognize and act on these impulses. When you need a buzz saw, don't keep grabbing a hammer.

If you're new to journaling, I hope you'll at least try putting pen to paper, even if it feels intimidating or uncomfortable at first. Not instead of any other tools that might be helpful, but in addition to them.

And for you, my tribe of dedicated analog journalers, we can get pretty specific about our practice. You may be devoted to a particular size of notebook, kind of paper, type of pen, color of ink, etc. Consider experimenting with new materials. Graph paper could be a revelation—who knows? Try all caps or your nondominant hand. Innovation over rigidity. Or challenge yourself and mix up the medium, as in this exercise.

PROMPT: *Chaos* and *stillness*. Draw, sketch, or doodle what each of these words mean to you, how they feel in your body, what they look like, or the kinds of environments you associate with each.

The point here isn't something to frame and hang on your wall. It's about confronting our own perceived creative limitations and getting comfortable with discomfort. Just like athletes need to build strength *and* stretch, staying flexible in our creative process can yield interesting, surprising results.

6

To Reread, or Not to Reread:

COST-BENEFIT ANALYSIS

My very first "bio photo" for the AllSwell website wasn't a picture of my face. Not only was I painfully uncomfortable in front of a camera at the time, I also didn't want my likeness to be too closely associated with this effort, which was then a side project. In case my existing clients came across it, I didn't want them to think my attention to their account was being diluted by a passion project. So I did what I considered to be the next best thing. I brought my lifetime's worth of journals to a photo studio, stacked them in piles in front of a seamless background,

Photo by Adam Guy

and a photographer friend snapped their beauty shot. I couldn't think of anything else as representative of my whole person than these dozens and dozens of filled books that I'd kept with reverence since the age of seven.

Eventually, I did need to take a photograph of my face, but this particular image was possible because I saved (and continue to save) all my journals. To me, there's something sacred about these books. I couldn't imagine tossing them in the rubbish bin. Someday, there might be one whopping big bonfire. Until then, I keep them stashed away in boxes. But I rarely, if ever, reread my filled notebooks. Within their pages, I released emotions one entry at a time and have moved on, better and lighter for it. Revisiting these pages seems about as appealing as going for a swim in toxic sludge.

Lots of people derive great benefit from reading their old journals. They value seeing where they were mentally and emotionally in the past, measuring it against where they are now, how they've changed, where they're stuck in looping patterns. For some, it's like getting to meet a version of their former, younger selves, and recognize what old pipe dreams they've been able to spin into reality. For these reasons and more, retaining and rereading an old journal can be assets for your creative and personal growth.

But if the idea of poring over your notebooks presents barriers to writing in them, just skip it. Visiting a former version of yourself can be anxiety producing. The construct of "writing for posterity" might imbue the act of journaling with intense and unnecessary pressure. Or it can stir up concerns (regardless of how unfounded they might be) about someone else using your words against you in the future. If any of the above ideas resonate, don't commit to rereading your pages down the road—or necessarily even saving them, the way I do. The journaling police won't bust you for neglect. On the contrary, you're paying attention to and honoring what's supportive for the development of your pen-to-paper practice. But what that looks like can change.

Not sure where you are on that spectrum? Here's a prompt to help.

PROMPT: How does the idea of rereading an old journal affect you? Are you curious, repelled, or excited about what you might find there? Some follow-up questions:

- If you have a strong emotional experience of not wanting to look at those pages, can you name the feeling and consider why you had that reaction and what it's made of?

- Is there a specific instance in which you did go back to an old entry, and it was helpful? What did you learn? Do you think you'd like to do that regularly, and if so, what kind of ritual or cadence would you like to set up for yourself?

- Do you like holding on to your filled notebooks, or does it add any kind of pressure, inhibiting your journaling? Where would you like to store your filled notebooks, or how would you like to release them?

Wherever you land, I recommend you stay in dialogue with yourself about your preferences instead of letting them harden into restrictions. Last summer, I was leading a digital workshop and grabbed one of my old journals off the shelf to use as a visual prop. I'd filled up this particular notebook a couple of years prior. While the group was busy writing in response to a prompt I'd provided, I started leafing through it. The voice I met there had a lot of relevant wisdom to share with my current self. I wasn't doing the backstroke in cringey toxic gunk; I was learning from and appreciating this person on the page. And I liked her.

I still don't tend to frequently reread my journals, but that day I dismantled yet another rule I'd set for myself. One that's no longer a fit for where I am today in my creative and personal development. So to address the common question of whether to revisit your old journals, the answer here is really up to you. If the concept stops you from writing in the first place, then it's counterproductive. But don't be afraid to meet your former self on the page, either. As I learned, you might really enjoy and benefit from what that version of you has to say.

7

External Stimuli:

SELF-GENERATED PROMPTS

The blank page can be an intimidating place to start. For some, it's wildly freeing to have that big, open expanse; for others, not so much. It's okay to crave a prompt, something to respond to. You're not alone, and you're not getting any demerits by asking for some external stimulation. In fact, I find idea generators to be a really useful tool in my own journaling. Prompts help me jump the track from my mind-chatter and access different topics, images, memories, and thoughts.

Like the English major I was, I tend to reach for books of poetry as jumping-off points. I arbitrarily open a book, read what's there, reflect on it for a beat or two. Then I write. I'm not penning an essay about the poem. It's not a pop quiz. Instead, I'm just making room for whatever sensations, concepts, or feelings arise and writing from that place.

Not into poetry? No problem. Any periodical will do. Here's how.

PROMPT: Flip open a book or magazine you have a connection to. Doesn't matter if it's *Sports Illustrated*, *The Economist*, or the Holy Bible. It could even be this book. Without giving it forethought, put your pointer finger down on the page. Read the word or phrase where it landed. That's your self-chosen prompt. Now, write that word on the top of a blank page of your notebook. What does it have to share with you? Why do you think that word found you today? Go.

I was working with a one-on-one creative coaching client who was a Rhode Island School of Design grad, a graphic designer by training, and a creative director by trade. This is one visually motivated individual. When I suggested the above, she said, "I am so not going to do that, Laura. It's not realistic for me." Fair enough. I asked her if she had any art monographs or books of photography around her home office. Yup. Okay, use them. Same situation, different medium. Open to any page. Look. Be present to the image. Witness whatever floats to the surface. What does it remind you of? Where does it take you? How does it make you feel? Write from there.

I encourage you to shake things up, identify sources for prompts that pique your interest, and use them in ways that speak to you. For instance, I shared the story above with one of AllSwell's digital groups. When we checked in at the top of the following session, a participant shared she was using her journaling commitment to spend time with the output of a specific painter. She'd been interested in exploring his work but hadn't otherwise made the space to do it—

until the idea was sparked by the visually inclined creative director. One reinterpretation led to another. Pretty cool. I love how people take a creative tool and make it their own. No matter what your jam may be—film stills, recipes, Polaroids, script excerpts, sculpture (heck, even memes)—the well of external prompts is endless. If you find an empty page to be daunting, grab hold of some external stimuli and start from there.

8

Rockstar Company:

ROAD TRIPS AND PUNK ROCK

You never know where breakthroughs might find you. For me, it happened in Cleveland. While, conceptually, I understood that much of the music that fuels our personal soundtracks originated in the pages of journals, it wasn't until I was standing in front of a display of notebooks with lyrics scrawled in them at the Rock & Roll Hall of Fame that I knew it to be true.

At the time, I was driving cross-country from Maine to Malibu with a friend and my dog. Our exact route was somewhat loose, but we'd agreed that, wherever we stopped, we'd do something unique to that location, sample some Americana. So there we were in Ohio, with a couple of hours to kill, and the Rock & Roll Hall of Fame called to us.

Interspersed between Greg Allman's Hammond organ; Alice Cooper's leopard-print, high-heeled boots; the very first Talking Heads T-shirt; and John Lee Hooker's guitar, I beheld exhibits of paper with words—lyrics—scrawled on them with varied degrees of urgency. It all began here, jotted down in cheap spiral notebooks, on yellow legal paper, hotel notepads, even matchbooks. It amazed me to see the handwritten language that became anthems sung in packed arenas.

Many of the songs we know by heart—the ones that exalt and comfort us—started with scribbled words. Loads of recording artists whose lyrics are woven into our collective cultural memories use the act of writing down their thoughts as an inherent part of their process. Punk, folk, pop, jazz, rock, rap, and more—a pen has fueled them all.

Putting pen to page fuels booty-shaking dance parties, ecstatic concerts, and all those tracks we sing out loud with the windows down. My friend and I put this knowledge to good use on our westward road trip. You can also tap music to freshen or deepen your mindful writing practice, no concert ticket required.

PROMPT: Pick a tune (whatever speaks to you) and listen with presence. Headphones come in handy here. Maybe close your eyes, to limit other sensory input, and focus on the music. You can tune into the lyrics, or not. Maybe you're hearing a phrase differently than any other time you've listened to this song because of the intent you're bringing to the process. Or instead of paying attention to the words, listen to the track as a whole, letting it wash over you. Pay attention to the physical feelings that emerge. What images, memories, or thoughts float into view? Open your notebook and write. It doesn't have to be in direct relation to the song. You're not reviewing the album for *Rolling Stone*. You're letting the piece of music become a portal into your own state of mind. Don't like where it takes you? That's okay. You have permission to pick another song. Start again.

I am old enough to remember making mixtapes for my friends. I spent hours crafting the perfect journey, song by song. When done, I'd customize the cassette wrapper with personalized drawings. It was an intimate exchange to swap mixtapes. I still love trading playlists with friends, in part because each of us has memories stored in songs. Maybe your first make out session, or some lyrics that spoke to you when nothing else could. The permutations are endless, so here's a prompt to help you wade into music-fueled meaning and nostalgia, one track at a time.

PROMPT: Make a list of songs on your life's soundtrack. What's on your personal playlist? What memories do you associate with each song? Why did you choose them?

While we're on the topic of how music and writing interact, I also suggest experimenting with using music as a backdrop for your journaling sessions. It can help transform a space by setting the mood. I've spent a lot of time honing playlists for AllSwell workshops, learning how to choose songs that support participants. Instrumental is good, but I avoid what I call "spa music." No pan flutes, unless that's your thing. This is your adventure, so turn the music up, put the metaphorical top down, and let in all that fresh inspiration.

Maybe sometime you'll choose to share a piece of what you write with the world, like those lyricists I came across in Cleveland. But that's not the point. It's engaging in the creative act that provides catharsis. Whatever your journaling practice looks like, know you're in the company of great artists and iconoclasts.

Every time you pick up a pen rather than numbing out in front of screens, you are engaging in nonconformist behavior. Which is why I say that journaling is very "punk rock."

9

Cut the Rut:

WHY JOURNALING WORKS FOR WORKING CREATIVES

On a rainy fall evening in New York City, I was leading an AllSwell workshop for a room full of "wellness lifestyle" journalists. You might think they'd be the ideal target to become apt journalers, eager to wring all the value out of putting pen to paper, but it was entirely the opposite. After a day spent writing and editing, the last thing they wanted to do was write some more. Most participants were there on editorial assignment or trying to stay current about the latest offerings and trends in the space. They were professional and polite, but I could tell they weren't personally into it.

Every group that gathers at the writing table is special, but the ones that are the hardest to convert, who sit down with arms crossed over their chests and mental barriers in place—those are my favorite workshops to lead. It's part of my job as a facilitator to identify and activate the right devices to turn the tide, enabling each participant to engage. When it happens, it's incredibly satisfying to see people who walked in the door with prejudices against the efficacy and worth of journaling light up with enjoyment at their own breakthroughs. This was one of those workshops.

And I understood why they weren't enthusiastic. When you're creative for a living, the idea of spending more time digging away at the same terrain doesn't necessarily fill you with a sense of excitement. It's like a "busman's holiday." Meaning, if you're a bus driver by trade, riding a bus on your days off doesn't exactly feel like a vacation. It can seem like more work. Plus, this particular segment of media gets pitched new health-optimization practices all day long. It's harder to excite them when their in-boxes and minds are already filled up with fanatical press releases.

I could certainly relate. I'd been them (and, as an occasional reporter, some days I still am). That provided a natural entry point. You tend to become a journalist because of a love of words, a fascination with telling stories, of unearthing new territory and sharing what you've found. But if you're good at it and decide to make this your vocation, you tend to shift away from the purity of that experience pretty quickly. You report stories in certain styles dictated by a given outlet; the tone has to match the publication; concessions must be made to advertisers; stories should be targeted for "engagement"; headlines devolve into clickbait, etc. Stick with it, and success often means you move up the masthead and away from editorial to managing other creatives and playing politics. You become engaged in the fragmented business of publishing rather than writing and reporting. As I shared this, workshop participants began nodding slowly in acknowledgment. Their body language changed, signaling a new openness to the process. So I pressed on, sharing that journaling provides a way to reclaim our creativity, to return to the raw act of putting words on paper, with no third-party gaze. No advertisers to please, no conversion stats or copy editor adherence. In fact, journaling implies no intended reader at all. Here you get the opportunity to return to what initially fueled your early desire to write, to explore a concept or idea on the page, to meander until you've had your fill.

This is true not just for journalists but for any flavor of working creative. Architects, photographers, industrial designers—it doesn't matter whether or not your craft is related to the written word; reconnecting with the essence of creativity minus a viewer, audience, or client via mindful journaling can be deeply nourishing. It helps refill the well we use every day in our output. Here's a prompt to help you connect with that dynamic.

PROMPT: When was the last time you were creative for the sake of creativity? Where were you? What was it? What inspired you, and how did it feel? Write or draw your answer.

After a decade plus of running the marketing and communications agency I founded, despite loving what I did for a living, I was burnt out on serving up my ideas for client judgment and approval. I'd also arrived at a point in the growth of the business that required me to spend more hours of my day managing up (clients) and managing down (employees) than actually doing the work that had drawn me to this profession in the first place. It was through journaling about this sense of loss that I realized I needed something that was just for me, a passion project where I could test out ideas and stretch creative muscles without external input. That was part of where the idea for developing a notebook brand came from. I figured I could gift them in business development meetings as a nice point of differentiation, a marketing line item for my primary revenue stream. At the time, I didn't imagine the full breadth of what it would become, but by journaling about my own burnout, I found a productive and exciting way forward.

I'm still in touch with some of the journalists who were at the writing table that night in New York City. They don't all journal regularly, but it's become a tool they can use to reinvigorate themselves, like a minivacation right there on the page. And it's available for you, too. The journaling equivalent of a weekend in the Caribbean, minus the cost and the sunburn.

10

Much More than Complaining:

JOURNALING FOR THE COLLECTIVE GOOD

"Never complain, never explain" might be a go-to public relations strategy for the British royal family, but for fostering mental well-being and creativity, it's worse than not helpful; it's destructive.[1] Dressed up as decorum, unyielding positivity, or even entrenched neutrality, can become a barrier between you and attaining flow state. Thankfully, you don't have to choose between toxic stoicism and hot mess. This isn't a binary.

Even if you're one of those naturally buoyant, chill individuals (you lucky duck), it's healthy if not vital to reevaluate your direction along the way. Even when things are swell, you can outgrow your own dreams and be ready for something else. For instance, I've had personal and professional goals which I attained and enjoyed. Things were humming along just fine. But since we aren't fixed points on a map, it eventually became time for me to make changes. Not because anything was wrong, but the status quo I'd built no longer lined up with the version of myself I'd become. The only way I had access to that awareness was by picking up a pen.

Giving ourselves permission to feel things can be daunting, but compartmentalization is not a long-term strategy for success. Writing through awkward periods of ambiguity and difficulty demonstrates strength and resourcefulness, not weakness. Journaling doesn't mean you're sitting in the emotional equivalent of dirty bathwater; on the contrary, you're letting it run down the drain.[2] Smarty-pants you is wisely using one of the available release valves.

Hesitant newbies share that they feel journaling can be self-indulgent navel-gazing. Taking time to contemplate your interior life is actually the opposite of being selfish or self-centered. You're acting in the best interest of your community. By reducing your own stress and anxiety via expressive writing, you'll be interacting with those around you as a better version of yourself, and your entire community will be better for it.[3]

PROMPT: Take this opportunity to grumble, moan, and protest as much as you want. Release it all in ink rather than having that plaque build up in your psychological arteries. A notebook is a refreshingly neutral space. Give yourself enough judgment-free time to exhaust the subject (or subjects). This isn't for posterity. You don't need to commit to feeling this way next week, tomorrow, or even in five minutes.

Once you complete the exercise, take a pause. Give it a few minutes or a few days. Then reread what you wrote. Has your perspective shifted? Are you still as activated, or has the combo of time and reflection helped ease the inflammation? Pick up your pen, and write about the experience of having generously given yourself the space to state whatever's been bugging you rather than holding it in.

Stashing unresolved distress under the proverbial couch doesn't work for very long. Those dust bunnies metastasize into dust elephants if they aren't given room to dissipate. Air them out.

But you don't need to stop there. A notebook is also a place to mobilize yourself (and others), to create action. If you're feeling stuck in a muddled, negative loop, your journal unlocks forward motion and clarity. When my interior emotional landscape feels more like a dumpster fire than a verdant meadow, this is what I do.

PROMPT: Organize your present concerns by listing them out. Now, number them from most annoying to least annoying. That might be enough to help you throttle back from the red zone and give you some awareness about the hierarchy of what's really bugging you. Often, it's not what you think it is.

What can you address now? That's your Tier 1. Put the others to the side as Tier 2 or 3, and stash them for a later date.

Apply some solution-based thinking to Tier 1. How can you either counter or transform any of these "knots," either partially or in their entirety? If there are items that seem dauntingly complex or are simply out of your control, ask yourself how you can adjust the ways you interact with that particular dynamic. Shifting how we respond to something is a powerful choice, too.

Applying structure provides clarity and gives you power over your circumstances. That dumpster fire? It's out. It might not be "meadow" status yet, but I'm headed in the right direction.

Life happens; some days will be complicated and challenging. And that's okay. Instead of being frozen in place, susceptible to breakage, you're mindfully writing your way to supple resilience. Maybe you started by "complaining on the page," but you are restoring optimism and agency in the face of difficulties. Paths emerge. You have options. Instead of white-knuckling it, pushing your problems away by force and will, you're teaching yourself how to counter conflict with increased mental agility and developing an ability to self-regulate your nervous system.

Typically, we don't have many safe, unjudging places to dive into inquiry, asking questions like, "How do I feel about this? Does it support my evolution? How can I transform these circumstances?" But the page is a deep pool, ready and able to receive all of you.

11

Journaling for Bros:

MORE MASCULINE SELF-EXPRESSION, PLEASE

Although I consider myself a girl's girl to my core, my status as a "groomsmaid" outpaces my tenure as a bridesmaid. On multiple occasions, I've been the sole female representation in a groom's bridal party. Asked by male friends to stand up with them before their community and whatever kind of god they believe in, I watched them say "I do" to the women of their dreams.

The groomsmaid dynamic is an atypical role in American culture—the female platonic best friend to a hetero male. Far from being a rom-com setup, it's a privilege. Because when things go south—and I mean get *really* bad—I'm often the only person these guys open up to.

As a woman I easily (over)share with my closest female friends. It isn't unusual for us to reach out to one another when we're having a tough time and disclose intimate details,[1] versus cisgender males, who often don't feel comfortable disclosing their interior life, prevented by a mix of stigma and stunted habits.[2] When the going gets really rough for them, there is so much cultural shame bound up in a display of emotional vulnerability that their challenges often are compounded by the experience of navigating them alone.

Some of the men dearest to me have suffered in near silence during difficult times. I could see something wasn't quite right but had to break down entrenched barriers to get them to communicate, exposing just how tender (and sometimes tenuous) things really were. But not every dude out there has that resource. They're unlikely to confide in their male buddies, wives, or girlfriends—and certainly not their colleagues or mentors—because they feel their suffering may be perceived as irrevocable weakness, something they absolutely cannot emotionally afford.

Over a decade ago, I had multiple marketing and communications clients in the male-dominated field of action sports. Between privately bearing witness to searing masculine pain, and the toxic, cartoonish bro-ism I was seeing at work, it was clear guys needed an outlet for releasing and processing their emotions. Like, for instance, a journal. Diving into research mode, I discovered just how beneficial journaling was *specifically for men.*

According to neuroscientist Dr. Matthew Lieberman, men tend to benefit more from writing about their feelings than women.[3] This is due to "the novelty factor" of journaling, and a perception that they don't have other outlets. Moreover, those positive effects are amplified for guys when they write in longhand. Lieberman conducted a study in which he discovered that writing about an emotional experience reduces activity in the amygdala, the part of our brains responsible for controlling the intensity of our emotions.[4] So the more cis men jot down about what's really eating away at them (regardless of whether a solution is identified), the less it will actually bother them. Effectively, it turns down the volume on their worries.

Let's support that process with a prompt for the guys, though the exercise would be beneficial for any of us.

PROMPT: What are some of the secrets you keep, and why? What role does holding in this information play in your life? Your answers might range from fairly casual ("my credit score is lousy"; "I bought a boat I couldn't afford to impress a woman who doesn't love me"; "I didn't get the promotion I was up for," etc.) to more intense terrain.[5] Let fresh air into those dark corners. For this exercise, six minutes is a solid place to start. But you may want to invest more time in this prompt, stretching to twenty when you're ready. If you're worried about privacy, ripping these pages up afterward might feel good and provide some somatic catharsis.

Follow-up steps:

- Reflect on your experience. How did it feel to write down/rip up your emotions?

- And now that you've done it, can you identify places or times of day that you might be more comfortable putting pen to paper in the future? Optimize your own process.

- Return to this prompt on a weekly basis for four consecutive weeks. You're learning how to consistently unburden yourself, rather than using up valuable subconscious energy on suppression.

- Consider resources that you could enlist to help support your ongoing excavation process, people and places that imbue a sense of safety.[6]

Since cis males are still more likely to be in positions of power and influence,[7] and less likely to seek out support (let alone journal) when they need it, getting more men to the page is not just about the guys; it helps us collectively. If a man is mentally unwell, masking dark emotions, it's probably going to affect everyone around him. The flip side? If they're emotionally fit, it's better for everyone.

So if you love a man—be it your son, brother, husband, lover, or friend—please encourage him to journal. Heck, maybe even give him a copy of this book so he knows where to start. Turn your dearest dudes on to the experience of writing mindfully. It's a powerful and dignified act, and it is likely to save someone you care about from unnecessary suffering.

And if you're reading this as a man in emotional pain, I invite you to see your notebook as a safe haven. Journaling is a demonstration of strength and protection because you're not just looking out for yourself; you're protecting the tribe. Everyone around you will benefit. Don't just take my "groomsmaid" word for it. Here's what the *Harvard Business Review* has to say on the topic: "The best thinking comes from structured reflection—and the best way to do that is keeping a personal journal."[8]

PART 2

Make Yourself Comfortable:

We're in Build Mode

Awe, boredom, nature, dopamine, and curiosity. These are some of the themes we dive into in Part 2. Now that you have gotten comfortable with the basics, here are some best practices to try on for size. You'll explore new and maybe unexpected ways to leverage a journal, for a better, more balanced you. Grow, baby, grow!

12

The Attention Economy:

COUNTERACTING "DIGITAL DUMBNESS"

It's not just you; we are all epically distracted. Our attention is being expertly commoditized, bought and sold by brands and businesses, yanking our focus from cue to cue. And our brains are plumb-tuckered as a result. This may be the Attention Economy, but paying attention for any sustained period has never been more challenging.

It turns out trying to do more than one thing at a time (e.g., shop and read, text and drive, watch television and answer emails, etc.) isn't cognitively feasible. Multitasking is a myth. More accurately, we "task-switch," flipping back and forth. And we do a lot of that in this economic and digital climate, even though our minds aren't wired that way.[1] Task-switching is a massive drag on brainpower, increasing the likelihood of human error.[2] We end up accomplishing less, and the end product isn't as reliable.[3]

It might seem antithetical, but monotasking—doing one thing at a time—is actually more productive. Initially, it can feel foreign, even uncomfortable, because we've gotten used to being on the receiving end of multiple simultaneous sources of input. Comparatively, sustained concentration on a single project or problem is good for our noggins.[4] You can use your journal as a way to counteract "digital dumbness," the mental exhaustion caused by ceaseless task-switching. Take this prompt for a spin whenever you're feeling fried.

PROMPT: Choose one sense (sight, sound, scent, taste, or touch/texture) and devote five minutes or more to observing what you are seeing, hearing, smelling, tasting, or feeling. Simply notice. Sift through the layers—sort of like a wine tasting, but instead of vino, it's a sensory examination of your environment in this present moment. Take sips. There are probably more obvious "top notes" and other, more subtle elements that might have eluded you if you hadn't taken this time to notice a single sense. What else is there? Jot it all down, without judgment.

When you're done, check in. Follow up with one or more of these bonus prompts on the page:

- Did sticking with one sense for the full amount of time feel stifling, or was there freedom in slowing down?

- Did you run out of things to write about, or were you able to push deeper because you had more time to devote to a single sense, uncovering a level of awareness that might have been hard to attain otherwise?

- Did you wish you'd picked a different sense at any point? Did you doubt yourself? Were you able to relax into the experience without critical chatter?

We aren't as apt to really take in our surroundings as we were before we had pervasive and portable smart devices. Being more aware of what's occurring right here, right now helps us become more mindfully present.

Repeatedly refreshing email, the lulling stream of TikTok amusements, and compulsively checking DMs are more than FOMO. They're handy avoidance tactics, delaying whatever it is we're trying to dodge (e.g., loneliness, boredom, anxiety, longing). And there's the paradox. The screens we're using to sidestep uncomfortable expressions of our humanness are exacerbating these challenging emotional states.[5] There's even an emerging disorder called nomophobia, separation anxiety from our devices and internet access.[6] You don't have to even be *interacting* with your phone—it can be in another room or building—and it's still negatively affecting your cognitive capacity.[7]

Spending time on the page is an antidote. It helps you carve out space from technology and, using intentional prompts (like the one here), it brings you back into present time and space.

PROMPT: Look around. Choose an object from your immediate environment. Pick something that your eye lands on, that seems to call for your attention. Just one. It could be obviously meaningful (your wedding ring) or kind of banal (a refrigerator). Look at it, contemplate it, take the time to actually see it. You can start by describing this thing—its nuances of color, shape, shadow, texture. You might notice the negative space between you and the item, which is kind of trippy and cool. Then tell its story. Objects hold meaning; they carry story and serve as receptacles for what we bring to them.

- What do you associate with the object?
- Why do you think you picked it?
- What/who/where does it remind you of?

Congratulations. Instead of tapping out, playing Candy Crush, or going down a Pinterest rabbit hole, you wrote a story about an object. You created meaning out of the mundane. You used your imagination. You were spontaneously creative.

Cultivating separation from technology takes practice. Try using this prompt when you might otherwise turn to a screen as an avoidance tool, staving off boredom or quelling nervousness. It's a great reason to have a notebook and pen in your bag, at the ready. This exercise gives you the opportunity to engage your own storytelling as a way to be *in* your life rather than numbing out and missing it.

We live in a noisy time, with bossy external voices taking up a lot of our mental real estate. There are quieter sources of wisdom available to us. They don't dominate or beg for our attention, but they might be more illuminating and interesting than what's readily available. It takes intent to tune into those subtler frequencies. Consider this: What would you think about if you weren't being told what to think about? What dreams could emerge out of that deliciously empty space? What questions would you ask? What calls to action would you come up with *for yourself*? Here's a three-part prompt to help you get at some of that good stuff.

PROMPT:

PART 1. What do you pay attention to? What voices, stories, friends, sources of information, be they external or internal (e.g., your intuition)? Are you engaging with them consciously or unwittingly? A helpful device is to scan a day, noting where your attention went. Give this process at least five minutes.

PART 2. Reread what you've written. What are you *not* paying attention to? To what degree are the key elements of how you define yourself—your core beliefs and values—present in your daily intake? To what extent are you making room for the quieter, important, but not urgent elements versus the cacophony of the urgent yet unimportant?

PART 3. Identify a source of information you value but don't regularly make room for. What (or who) is it and why? Some examples might include the natural world, differing opinions, your intuition, your body, a more global news source, your mother's advice.

You're now poised to better prioritize a voice that hasn't gotten enough of your beautiful attention lately because it isn't "noisy." Mary Oliver wisely counsels, "Attention is the beginning of devotion."[8] We get to choose who and what we're devoted to. It's not merely a matter of economics; it's sacred territory.

13

Happy Hour:

AND I DON'T MEAN MARGARITAS

A brush with mortality at a young age raised my bar, and by that I am referring to the quality of life that I was determined to cultivate. Having weathered aggressive breast cancer in my early thirties, I didn't just want to "survive." I wanted an upgrade. I began voraciously researching ways to increase my physiological health, which I'd just fought so hard to sustain. In the process, I learned one's emotional state isn't wholly determined by circumstances; we actually get a say in how we feel.[1] This seemed revelatory at the time, as I was emerging from a fear-based victim paradigm and knew that wasn't how I wanted to move through the world anymore. One of the easiest ways to impact our frame of mind is activating our innate creativity. Enter: your journal.[2] We can harness our neural chemistry to lighten our mood by putting pen to paper.

Less constructive, quick-fix mood boosters come saddled with downsides, like add-to-cart endorphins followed by credit card bill hangovers. If you want to feel better fast—minus unpleasant side effects—here's an interest-free exercise to help access your own, personal "happy hour."

PROMPT: Write a "like list." Not a *love* list; that's higher stakes. Just stuff that you dig, things that you enjoy, moments that provide a little hit of delight. Maybe they're part of your everyday life, or maybe they're more of a special occasion type thing, or a mix. Here are a few of my current low-key likes to help you identify your own:

- Naming my plants. Currently: Jaime, Myrtle, and Maria Callas—who is beautiful but a bit of a diva.

- Watering said plants.

- Silky, cooling, cotton-sateen-weave sheets in the summer and sliding into fluffy flannel sheets in the winter.

- A bowl of freshly popped popcorn with sea salt *and* ground pepper.

- Hailing a black cab in London.

- Stone fruit season.

- Finishing an issue of *The New Yorker* the same week it arrives. (Rare.)

- An outdoor shower.

- Mailing a letter.

- The first few amorphous bars of a song at a live rock show, followed by the moment when everyone seems to collectively recognize the song and cheers.

- Turning off lights around the house at the end of the night.

When making your list, try thinking of all five senses—sights, sounds, scents, tastes, and textures. Four minutes of writing provides a good base; add more minutes for more mojo. The longer you do it, the more opportunity you are giving your brain to enjoy the experience.

Notice how this shifts your mood. Are you smiling? Thought so. Rinse and repeat whenever you're feeling glum. On an ongoing basis, stretch to find new things to add rather than reverting to repetition.

This activity sounds straightforward, but that's not always the case. If reading the instructions didn't inspire you, that in and of itself can be good intel. I used this "like list" prompt as a warm-up at a workshop I led for high-level executive women. When I checked in after the exercise, one of the participants offered that this had been really difficult for her to consider. She realized that, for the past several years, most of her energies had been focused on the preferences and desires of others: the hundreds of employees she manages and her family. She couldn't readily come up with anything when thinking about it for herself. She didn't even know what she liked anymore. This was a powerful takeaway, and she vowed to both identify what was on her list and to make sure she was incorporating it into her life more and more.

This deceptively simple prompt is effective because our imaginations are remarkably powerful. They're so nuanced and effective that the "movies" we create in our minds impact how our bodies actually feel. Our brains send out neurochemicals, which correlate to the scenarios we're dreaming up. Anxious? Cortisol invokes a fight-or-flight response to get us the heck out of harm's way.[3] Cozy and loved? That's yummy, purring oxytocin.[4] Experiencing a sense of accomplishment? Swaggering dopamine has entered the building.[5]

Our bodies can't tell the difference between whether we're imagining something or if it's actually occurring. For example, if you've got a massive fear of great white sharks with bad dispositions and you inexplicably find yourself on a fishing boat, you're likely to have an elevated heart rate, be extra sweaty, and maybe experience shaking and shortness of breath as if Jaws himself were lurking under the surface—even if the number of bloodthirsty, psychotic sharks in the water is exactly zero. Your reactions have nothing to do with the actual presence of psycho sharks, but are in response to the *idea* of them.

Good news: The opposite is also true. The placebo effect is one of my favorite drugs. By simply focusing on (and writing about) positive ideas, experiences, and images, you can brighten up and actually *become happier*. These events don't even need to be happening here and now. Simply by writing about them, you're giving yourself an endorphin cocktail. Stirred, not shaky. Here's another mood-changing "happy hour" exercise to explore.

PROMPT: Choose a memory of a sunrise or sunset that's meaningful to you. Where were you? Who were you with? How old were you? Transport yourself into that place and time. Was it chilly and you were bundled up, or maybe was it height-of-summer hot and your skin was suntanned and salty? Were you standing or sitting? Were you drinking or eating anything? What did it feel like to be there, and in what ways is this particular sunrise or sunset significant?

I suggest you give yourself enough time to wander around in the memory, six minutes or more. But if you're really pressed for time, even four minutes can provide a minireset.

Notice that I didn't ask you to write about the Happiest Moment of Your Life. That's a pretty intense request to make of yourself. But spending time recollecting any positive memory, especially one that connects you to nature, is an easy way to turn on the serotonin tap and have a good soak.

Being able to impact your mood is about a lot more than having a sunny disposition. There are bottom-line reasons to try to be less bummed. Workplace research shows that employees with a positive disposition outperform negatively minded employees, optimistic salespeople outperforming their pessimistic colleagues by up to 37 percent. In a professional setting, this "happiness advantage" results in lower turnover rates and reduced organizational health care costs. Even medical doctors are three times more creative and 50 percent more accurate at diagnosing patients when in a positive mind-set.[6] Happier does in fact mean healthier, and that's good for business.

I'm not suggesting we should all be permanently upbeat. When things go terribly, profoundly wrong, I certainly don't pretend to be thriving. False positivity can feel like self-abandonment in the face of a list of struggles that are, indeed, real. Instead, I urge you to honor and process your own experience by speaking with trusted friends and/or connecting with a professional. And, yes, writing it out on the page.

But you needn't be miserable to tap into the benefits of putting pen to paper. If you only associate journaling with times of grief, disillusionment, or heartbreak, you're missing out. Of course, it's there for you during all those inky, midnight blue circumstances. But a journal is also an easy-to-access feel-good tool when you're hovering somewhere around "meh" and just looking for a lift. And over time, using it to cultivate a more positive mind-set helps us perform better in the face of legitimate hard challenges when they arise. You're not just making today better by embracing your personal creative aperitivo time; you're also setting yourself up favorably for all your tomorrows.

14

Any Tree Will Do:

AWE, SHUCKS

Sometimes, I am just so over myself. When I want to jump the track of my usual mind-chatter, those annoying looping reels of difficulties, desire, and stories, I know it's time to get outside.

Nature induces a state of awe, which results in a diminished focus on the self, increased empathy and prosociality (behavior intended to benefit others), and a heightened sense of meaning.[1] Instant reset. I can speak from multiple first-person experiences. Here's one: Witnessing the soaring, vibrant red stone arches at twilight in Arches

National Park served up a heaping portion of reverence. I went silent, gobsmacked by the vibrant, multistory geological formations that rose up in every direction. It was as if my eyes didn't have the capacity to take in all the majesty around me. This environment seemed to supersede the limitations of sight. My travel buddy kept saying, "Why didn't anyone tell us?" as if we were being let in on some divine secret. I felt both comfortingly insignificant and intimately connected to a palpable sense of beauty on a scale I'd rarely experienced before. I was elated, but also calmly present.

While immersive experiences like being awestruck in Moab offer heightened effects, you don't need to be exploring wilderness to recalibrate your connection to nature (and derive its benefits). Any tree will do. In this breathlessly fast-paced time, it's helpful to contemplate a tree. After all, they do most of the things we all do—communicate, respirate, replicate, make sacrifices, learn, and grow. They just do them *much* more slowly.[2]

PROMPT: Go sit by a tree, or pick a tree from memory. Write the story of that tree.

- What has it witnessed? What changes, animal interactions, human storylines has it seen? What role has it played?

- Did someone plant it? If so, who do you think they were, and why did they put this tree here?

- What has it lived through? How many rainstorms, sunny days, snowfalls, moonless midnights, first lights?

- Why do you think you chose this tree? What meaning does it hold for you, if any?

Trees have been on this planet for over 385 million years, preceding man and even dinosaurs.[3] So yeah, they've seen a thing or two. I find spending time contemplating that kind of constancy to be reassuring, especially against the backdrop of the breakneck speed of our business as usual.

As a mostly city kid, I used to believe nature was a place you visited, like a museum. It was usually accessed via a planned activity, like going to Central Park for the afternoon or a day trip to the beach. But that limited perspective denies the essential truth that nature is here, all around us, twenty-four hours a day—even in the most institutional, man-made settings.

If you have some version of my former "out there somewhere" perspective of the natural world, this prompt helps readjust your lens. A nature scan enables you to tap a steadying connection to the natural world at any time. The more counterintuitive the location, the more I appreciate this exercise.

PROMPT: Wherever you are, scan your space and identify items from the natural world—animal, vegetable, and mineral. It could be the fruit in a bowl on your kitchen counter, a plant on your desk, a bird outside your window, the dog resting at your feet, even the lettuce in your fridge, the coffee in your mug, or the sandwich in your belly. Now, peek under the surface of your environment. The wooden framing of a house, the metal girders in a high-rise, double-paned glass windows that exist to divide in from out, even particleboard—they're all derived from natural elements. List out what you're able to spot. Did you notice something in a new way? How does being aware of this natural network make you feel? Scan and explore. I suggest giving yourself at least six minutes in order to surprise yourself with your findings.

When I take the time to cast my eyes around my space, my

imagination slipping behind walls, I have incredible levels of appreciation for the awe-inducing number of ways nature supports humanity in general and me specifically. The library desk where I'm sitting as I write was made possible by trees. The sweater I'm wearing is made of the wool of an alpaca. Even my laptop is comprised of over thirty different minerals that have been extracted from the earth.[4]

This exercise is a fast track to awe, one of the most powerfully healing human emotions, but nature's contributions to our mental and physical health extend well beyond even awe. If you need to problem-solve or overcome a creative block, get yourself to a park. Time spent in nature refreshes our brains, making space for new tasks such as ideating.[5] We're also able to better concentrate, adapt to information, and respond to dynamic situations. Even our memory improves. Add to this list of upsides an energizing sense of vitality and a better mood.[6] Nature makes us more curious and imaginative versions of ourselves.[7] If you're looking for your muse, she's probably climbing a tree or out rooting around in a garden.

I've been honored to facilitate mindful writing workshops in some truly epic outdoor settings: in a grove of Mendocino redwoods; perched on driftwood logs around a fire on the beaches of Vancouver Island; in a breezy, open-air palapa in Zihuatanejo, Mexico; by a freshwater stream in upstate New York; on multiple lush Hawaiian islands; and so many more. I'd be remiss if I didn't call out our role in preserving these places, as well as addressing the overall health of our planet. Creativity and innovation are key tools necessary to problem-solve our collective way to the other side of any crisis. And you know where to go to renew your ability to dream up large-scale solutions: the same natural settings we're looking to save are our saviors. All of this is to say, go outside and play. And take a journal with you.

15

Get Wet:

BEACH AND BATH BENEFITS

"Beach brain." While this is certainly not a technical term, for me it refers to a lovely, hazy state of calm joy. When I spend a day at the beach, my worries shrink, anxiety lifts, and what's left is a version of myself that I like a lot. She's chill, smiles easily, and feels connected to something much bigger than daily striving. What's real is what's right here—the sand under my feet, the vista in front of me, the sound and colors of the water, the comforting repetition of waves.

All of that feels so good because water (particularly salt water) is offering us its multisensory support:

- *Sight:* Humans have a bias toward creativity[1] and comfort[2] around the color blue.[3]

- *Sound:*[4] Hearing natural waterscapes, such as lapping waves and rainstorms, contributes to a relaxed, parasympathetic state.[5]

- *Air:* The "waterfall effect,"[6] which occurs when droplets of water break apart aerodynamically (such as in tumbling surf or a heavy downpour), changes the electrical charge in the air.[7] Breathing in this negatively charged air helps reduce symptoms of depression and increases relaxation while activating our ability to process information.

- *Absorption:* The mineral content of salt water and naturally occurring hot springs enhances tranquility and boosts cognition.[8]

Corona's marketing team had it right when they equated the Mexican lager with unhurried vacation days and added a soundtrack of gentle surf to their commercials. Even if you can't park yourself at the water's edge, you can access some of its positive connotations (and effects) via your imagination and a journal. No beach, no problem. Here's a water-themed prompt designed to help bring yourself into a parasympathetic state.

PROMPT: "What is your favorite body of water and why?" No need to limit yourself to spots on the globe in your response. It can be a river or a lake, but also a bathtub or your teapot. Explore your connection with water, writing for six minutes.

My go-to response is a stretch of beach in Montauk, specifically in June when the beach roses come into bloom. The combination of intermingling scents (floral and briny) and contrasting colors (deep pink petals, bright green flora, blue sky and water) is a unique sensory snapshot. Lingering mentally in that space and time on the page is like teleporting me there for a few blissed-out moments.

This prompt has been answered in myriad different ways over the years in workshops. While I absolutely never require participants to share their answers, people often volunteer the unique places to which the question took them. A *Sports Illustrated* swimsuit model said her favorite body of water was her kitchen sink, where she bathed her infant son. A pro surfer didn't cite a favorite spot for perfect waves; instead, it was the water in each of her cells. Others have shared cedar soaking tubs, rivers, outdoor showers, cenotes, quarries, lagoons, fishing holes, hot springs, mugs of steaming tea, creeks, and swimming pools. My many years of posing this prompt and witnessing the spectrum of interpretations have convinced me that we are as varied as we are similar. Be it choppy or still, running from a tap or a stream, we are unified in our response to this element of the natural world.

Wherever you can connect with water, go there. Bring along the awareness of all the ways it wants us to be our healthiest and most innovative selves. Dump some Epsom salts into a tub or sit quietly by a reservoir; even gazing at the reflections in a puddle can offer up a doorway. Crack a journal, and see what comes to the surface. No sand in sight? Not to worry. You might just slip into beach-brain mode anyway.

16

Dopamine Push-Ups:

DON'T CHASE DINNER DURING LUNCH

I was at a friend's exquisite oceanfront home on a summer afternoon, taking in the beautiful water view from a lounge chair. Not too shabby. Anchored in the cove out front was a yacht, with bathing-suited people out on deck. I wistfully thought, *Wouldn't it be nice to be out on a boat right now?* That, my friends, is dopamine talking. I was suddenly no longer appreciating the moment I was in, what I had; I was mentally trading up. And I'd bet the people on that boat were looking at this gorgeous property thinking, *Wouldn't it be amazing to have such an incredible beach house, where this was your view every morning?* Yacht or mansion, we still tend to want more, thanks to dopamine.

It doesn't matter how massive your hotel suite might be; this neurotransmitter would have us perpetually on the lookout for an upgrade. Have a first-class ticket? You want to fly private. But when your neighbor at the hangar has a Gulfstream that's newer than yours, you start hankering for a faster jet. Basically, "I need a bigger yacht" is dopamine whispering in your ear. This hormone can distract us from enjoying what we have, yanking us out of the present, and pointing us toward the next and the new in a never-ending quest of unchecked capitalism.

We get a dopamine hit not from having but *getting*. And there's no finish line to this exhausting race.[1] It can derail us from what's actually beneficial, driving us instead to be mindlessly reckless in big and small ways. It's the main chemical culprit for why we overspend, overeat, and scroll endlessly.

So why do we have it in the first place? It's part of a primal survival system. Dopamine helped our ancestors pay attention to sources of sustenance (e.g., berries in the bushes), so we could earmark them as important. In times of scarcity, dopamine served our evolutionary impulse. Today we are awash in options, culinary and otherwise, but we are still neurologically triggered by every new "berry." Social media, in particular, harnesses this dynamic to keep us wholly engaged.[2] In this state, we are a lot like the Cookie Monster, unconsciously chomping our way through a steady stream of pleasure centers, yet unable to actually enjoy any of them.

But dopamine isn't inherently bad. This "reward center" hormone can be a total superstar when it's balanced. It helps our motor functions and our ability to focus and self-motivate; it even stabilizes mood. It's when dopamine levels are off-kilter that it can cause havoc. Too little and we're more likely to fall prey to unsavory sources. Too much and things that used to feel good no longer neurologically register, so the chase for more intensifies.[3]

With this as context, here's a writing cue to consider.

PROMPT: How do you think dopamine tends to drive you? Try doing a scan from morning till night. Where do you see this dynamic show up in your daily behavior?

This prompt isn't intended to be a tsk-tsk exercise. Being aware of the dopamine dynamic in your life can be extremely empowering. Once you understand the reason for the impulse toward newer and shinier—and why it feels so darn important—you gain valuable metacognition (understanding of your own processes), an uptick in self-awareness. For instance, you won't necessarily become less ambitious. But you can more closely consider your ambitions and determine whether those objectives really serve you, or whether you're operating in service of dopamine. It might be time for a tweak or two.

One way to balance your dopamine-centric urges is to do what I call dopamine push-ups. Create your own reward center. This helps you take control of your neural chemistry, so your attention is less prone to get snagged on lesser sources of dopamine. I've paired some science-backed options with commonsense examples to get you rolling.

- *Embrace kiddo-style creativity.*[4] Pick a project and give yourself the chance to create without boundaries or rules. Go to an art store and treat yourself to whatever materials speak to you. Then go have flow-state fun while making a beautiful mess.

- *Get uncomfortable.* Challenge yourself to a "painful pursuit," such as taking an ice bath, going camping (glamping doesn't count, sorry), or a cold blast in the shower.[5] If you're on the shy side, talking to a stranger counts. The point is to go outside your comfort zone.

- *Connect with community.*[6] Call a friend, see a buddy, or plan a day trip across town to spend time with someone you love but don't see as often as you'd like.

- *Get outdoors.* Spend some time in nature, especially activities that expose you to sunlight, including beach walks, planting a garden, or jumping in a lake for a swim.

- *Declutter.* Simple and satisfying, purging provides a sense of accomplishment. Pick a drawer or a section of your closet and have at it! Pro tip: Choose a space small enough that you can finish the project within two hours or less to bypass possible overwhelm. An achievable goal is key.[7]

- *Move your body.*[8] Break a sweat by going for a walk, hitting the gym, or heading to a workout class. Bonus dopamine points if it's an activity you haven't done before (see below).

- *Take mini-adventures.*[9] Harness the novelty of the new, even if it's something simple like trying out a different cuisine or restaurant, exploring a new bookstore, trying out a recipe, surfing a different spot, or taking the scenic way home.

Now that you're well stocked with some samples, here's a prompt to explore.

PROMPT: Create a routine of dopamine push-up options that appeal to you, ranging from readily available (quick and easy) to more complex ones that require some advance planning. This doesn't mean climbing Kilimanjaro—more like camping with your kids in your own backyard. Choose activities that slot into the flow of your usual weekly schedule. What are some mini-adventures that you're curious about or creative projects you're keen to explore? Who are some people you'd like to see more of, or maybe a friend you could catch up with over coffee or on the phone?

Your menu is laid out, and you can tick your way through it, providing yourself with a healthy flow of dopamine. As a result, you'll be less likely to turn into the mindlessly munching Cookie Monster. Metaphorically, dopamine is scheming how to score a sought-after reservation for dinner while we're still eating our lunch. Personally, I want to enjoy my damn good tuna melt, not be mentally out the door and down the road, chasing a bowl of truffle pasta. The truffles can wait. Every bite is worth savoring.

17

Times Two:

MEDITATION + JOURNALING

Duos are winning. Popcorn and a movie. The beach and a bonfire. Shampoo and conditioner. Each part is good, but together they're better. This also goes for meditation and journaling. When combined, they're like brushing and flossing for your beautiful brain.

The relationship between the two is a topic that sometimes pops up in workshops. Do you need to do both? Is one more important? Is there a correct order? If you're curious, rather than taking a strict, dogmatic approach, my recommendation is to experience how they inform one another. This is one more way to explore your mindful writing practice.

If you're already a meditator, great. This means you'll be habit-stacking: layering a positive new practice on top of an existing one. The linked association makes it more likely for you to become a consistent journaler.[1] Whatever form of meditation you're into (guided, mantra-based, transcendental, walking, or—my personal favorite—meta "loving-kindness" meditation), fold in some mindful writing as a complementary amplifier.

If you're not sure how to begin meditating, you can try out one of the myriad apps available, but please remember that you don't need to engage with a screen to meditate. The earliest written records of meditation are from the Hindu Vedas, dating back to around 1500 BCE.[2] It's an ancient operating system.

I am certainly not a meditation expert, but here's a simple sequence I employ myself. To begin, try sitting quietly and noticing your breath flowing in and out. Let thoughts float through your awareness without engaging with them. You're not trying to stamp out your thoughts. Just bear witness and let them go. If you get tripped up, just give yourself some grace and return to the breath. That's all you need. Like journaling, meditation is, at its core, a self-paced curriculum that travels light. Just like a full tank of gas and a great playlist, this duo will take your journey further and make it more enjoyable.

As for which to do first, there's plenty of benefit in both directions.

Meditate, then journal: By tacking journaling onto the end of your meditation, you give yourself space to remember and explore whatever may have emerged during your session. A "sticky" thought, an emerging idea, a feeling, or even a frustration can become the basis for valuable reflection. Jotting it down means it won't get lost in the daily mind clutter of distractions. You have the option of revisiting your entry later, continuing to build out your contemplation on the page.

Journal, then meditate: Even a brief meditation before journaling can be centering, offering a more grounded perspective. I think of it as clearing away the debris "brush" so I can see the outline of the trees. The combo yields a fertile expanse for breakthrough writing, a way to fast-track past chattering "monkey mind" banter.

If you're a newbie to all of this, it's all right to go slow. No need to hurl yourself into a full Vipassana retreat. Let's ease in with The Fives.

PROMPT: Today, free-write for five minutes, then meditate for five minutes. Tomorrow, switch it up. Meditate for five, then (you guessed it) write for five. Notice how one practice informs the other. Observe, play, see what works for you. Try doing it five days a week. Aim for five weeks, gradually adding a minute to each practice per week. By the end, you'll land at ten minutes of meditation and ten minutes of journaling—a solid mindfulness practice. Congratulate yourself. Smile.

18

Victory Lap:

WELL DONE (LIST)

After they win a race, Formula 1 drivers often acknowledge their accomplishment by going around the track one more time at reduced speed. This gives them an opportunity to celebrate their triumph, something we do little of in daily life.

My clients often share that they feel as if their lives have become a treadmill without a stop button, and they're constantly playing catch up. The "race" doesn't end. They have a perception they're falling short when it comes to taking care of their mental, physiological, and creative well-being. While they never stopped setting (and accomplishing) goals, they rarely take time to reflect on a job well done. Journaling can help carve out that time. This prompt is designed to take you off that treadmill and make space for you to feel good about what you've already achieved.

PROMPT: If, like me, you map out your to-do list at night, this activity becomes a precursor. Before you look forward, look back. Take a beat to reflect, noting the ways you looked after yourself today.

Jot down even the smallish stuff that you did to take good care of yourself. Here's a real-life example from my own notebook sometime in the dark days of February:

- Used my seasonal affective disorder light in the morning
- Fit in a quick workout
- Called my mom
- Exceeded my steps goal
- Took my vitamins—*allll of them*
- Researched the benefits of parallel play
- Returned those ugly boots (I'm bad at e-commerce)
- Brought home big camellia branches to flower indoors
- Didn't look at screens for an hour before bed
- Reduced monthly banking fees

- Refilled humidifier at night instead of ignoring that it's empty and waking up dry as the Sahara

As you can see, nothing here is winning me any awards. But in making that list, I thought, *Dayum, I take pretty good care of myself.* I gifted myself a dopamine hit for being a good steward of my own person. It was a little victory lap, which then helped me stay motivated to keep going. This prompt also encourages you to "crowd out" negative influences, a concept I'm borrowing from nutritionists.[1] The more healthy choices you make, the less space there is for activities that are the equivalent of junk food (e.g., binge scrolling).

Most of us aren't taught how to accept a compliment, let alone appreciate our own accomplishments. Instead, it's on to the next, the next, the next. Let's slow down and recognize good work, even if it's on a granular level. This prompt provides a way to get used to quietly patting ourselves on the back. Nice work, kid.

Try out a "done list" before your to-do's and see how it shifts your perspective. Rather than instant overwhelm, you're starting from a positive set point, which can fuel you to be more ambitious and visionary as you identify your goals for the day/s ahead. Of course, your "done list" will look different than mine, but I believe you'll get a similar kick of satisfaction as you claim some small wins along the way to your big (and biggish) triumphs.

19

Welcome Home (to Your Body):

NONTOXIC AWARENESS

I admit, I hesitated when contacted by nonprofit Keep A Breast, an organization that educates young people about breast cancer, to create and lead an original mindful writing workshop for their upcoming survivors' retreat. As a young survivor myself, I was one of the luckiest ones—no recurrences, and I'd been pronounced cured several years prior. As much as this invitation was a profound honor, it was also a heavy challenge, chockablock with potential personal triggers, including a fast track to a megadose of survivor's guilt. Despite not wanting to revisit such tender terrain, it was an opportunity to sift through my own gnarly experiences and use them to help others. So I put my big girl pants on and dug in.

Even if you don't have to cope with a health crisis, many (maybe most) of us have a complicated relationship with our bodies. The body is fraught territory. While I crafted these exercises for my survivor sisters with illness in my rearview mirror, I've since used them repeatedly for lots of different groups, including men. We all store information in our cells, and if we listen in, they have a whole bunch of helpful information to communicate. It doesn't matter what kind of equipment you've got under the hood; your body will thank you.[1]

PROMPT: Pick a body part you like or appreciate. It can be an internal organ such as your lungs, or your skin, teeth, wrist, neck, whatever. We have so many beautiful parts to pick from, each quietly accomplishing so much. What is that part's "job"? What does it do for you? What memories do you associate with it? Why do you think you picked this limb or organ? Spend four or five minutes appreciating this particular physical aspect of yourself on the page.

Move your gaze around and try out different spots on and in your body. Maybe instead of your "hands" in their entirety, pick just one finger and consider what its role is, what meanings you ascribe to it.

I'm not playing favorites, but I love this prompt and have personally gotten a lot out of it. Each time I return to it, I find some new aspect of my physical form to celebrate. I once chose "spleen" because I realized I had no idea what it did. I've been carrying this thing around since I was in utero, yet I had zero clue what its actual function was. I looked it up, and based on what I found, I thoroughly and profusely praised my spleen on the page for being so cool.

(BTW: It turns out that spleens are really rad. They clean your blood, filtering out damaged red blood cells. They're also like a little house where all the white blood cells live, and when the body sounds the alarm because there's an infection or virus lurking, the spleen lets the white cells know, "Okay, guys. It's time to get out there and fight!"[2])

Every time I've recovered from a cold or flu, that's the spleen. Whenever a cut or scrape heals up, it's the spleen doing its thing. It deserves way more gratitude than I'd previously awarded it. Had I not taken this prompt for a spin, I might've lived the rest of my days without this knowledge and new appreciation for a piece of my corporal being.

Taken singly, this exercise might not yield a paradigm-busting revelation. You're probably not going to talk about your newfound spleen revelations at a dinner party. (Or maybe you will?!) But when the prompt is done repeatedly, cumulatively, I find there's a kind of wonder that emerges. It's a balm for the messages of perfectionism that are running laps through our minds. Rather than mentally chopping up our appearance into bits for critical evaluation, a new, nontoxic relationship to the body coalesces. It can offer up profound relief.

I remember emerging from the hospital after my first breast cancer surgery, still in an anesthetic haze. Out on the sidewalk, back in my own clothes and in the fresh air, I did some mildly hysterical laugh-crying. Not because I was afraid or grateful (though yes, those too). I turned to my sister-in-law and said, "Five pounds. I cannot believe I ever cared about five pounds." It was only when confronted with my own mortality that I was able to see and dismiss the outrageous levels of body-dysmorphic cruelty I'd been imposing on myself for years. But you don't need to be pushed into that kind of tight corner to quiet internal judgments. You can journal your way there instead.

Much of the time, we treat our bodies like dogs, expecting them to perform on command—sit, stand, roll over, go fetch me a latte. From a health perspective, we tend not to even notice them (unless something's amiss), let alone hear their messages. So, let's tune in.

PROMPT: Drop into your skin and *embody your body*. Write a letter from your body to yourself. What does it want to say? Maybe it's a letter of gratitude, letting you know what a great job you're doing at staying hydrated, exercising, and taking your vitamins? Or it could be telling you to rest up and slow down. Perhaps it wants more time to play, run wild, and have fun. Write for seven minutes and see what shows up. Bear in mind, your letter may meander and not stick to a single narrative.

Reread your letter. Follow-up prompts:

- Did that feel good or was it uncomfortable?
- Was there a theme that emerged?
- Did anything surprise you?
- Now that you have this information, what steps do you want to take to respond to your body's letter?

Our brains aren't the only source of intelligence we have available. For instance, there's research emerging that the lining of our gut has millions of neurons, communicating instantaneously with the brain via a neural network that entirely bypasses the bloodstream.[3] And our aphorisms about intuition reflect that: "Gut reaction." "Trust your gut." "Gut feeling." Learning to hear and trust those impulses may take some pen-to-paper practice for those of us who aren't used to being in communication with our subtler selves. But science is catching up to what our bodies have known all along. You might even call it a homecoming.

20

Boredom Is Underrated:

SHUSHING POST-INDUSTRIAL STATIC

I'm a cheap date when it comes to surfing. I don't need perfectly formed, head-high waves to have a fun session. Almost anything is better than nothing in this context. With that low a bar, it was safe to think I was going to paddle out on a particular Monday morning, but when I rolled up to the parking lot and took a look, there were literally no waves. It wasn't even worth pulling my board out of my truck. I was extra-disappointed because this was a rare weekday morning I'd taken off work. And a warm, uncrowded, sunny beach day at that. But the ocean is in charge, and she had other plans. Deprived of my favorite dopamine fix, I pouted before I pivoted.

What I didn't do: Because it was a day off, I steered clear of digital notifications that might tug me into my in-box. I also didn't fire off text messages to quickly make a substitute social plan. I didn't book a tennis lesson. I didn't check yoga class schedules.

What I did: I spread my towel on the sand. I looked out at the horizon line. I took in the warming heat of the sand under me. I closed my eyes and eavesdropped a bit on the families settling their kids in at the beach, which brought a trickle of comforting nostalgia. I pulled a notebook out of my bag, and I jotted down what I was seeing, hearing, and feeling. This wasn't so bad. I was having a nice little morning, slow but sweet. I wrote, "Swell or no swell, all's well." And that's where the idea that would become AllSwell found me. This phrase was a key part of what propelled me to create a non-prescriptive approach to journaling. If everything had lined up the way I'd hoped, I wouldn't have been in such a receptive, undistracted state. Where a plan failed, a new adventure started.

Linguistically, boredom didn't have its current connotation until the Industrial Revolution.[1] Prior to that, our ancestors were too busy securing basics like food and shelter. But highly repetitive factory work yielded a kind of monotony that didn't exist before. And with many of life's daily tasks becoming mechanized (cranking up a car engine versus caring for horses, flipping on electric lights versus lighting candles and filling oil lamps, etc.), much of humanity experienced an excess of time and a corresponding experience of ennui.

I recognize that actively cultivating boredom sounds antithetical to a good time, but it actually helps reset our brains so we can better appreciate and enjoy experiences. When a mind is constantly stimulated, it requires heightened levels of arousal just to attain equivalent levels of engagement. Without restorative lulls, our senses become dulled. It's an addiction pattern, craving increased intensity to stave off boredom—like starting out playing backgammon with a buddy but ending up needing high-stakes roulette in a noisy casino just to generate the same level of enjoyment, or playing *Grand Theft Auto* when Wordle used to do the trick.

When it comes to creativity, absorbing external stimuli can be a great tool to jump-start a brainstorming session, but don't miss out on the generative power of a void. When we're deprived of a whole bunch of external input, our imagination kicks into gear, and we think in new, different ways.[2] Besides, we aren't meant to operate at maximum intensity at all times. I enjoy an espresso, but sometimes chamomile is the right call. Without valuable pauses to let our brains reset, we don't have a chance to "land" and have a look around, to ask and answer basic questions about our preferences, let alone birth an idea or two. And that's one of the reasons that putting pen to paper can be such a helpful ally. Your hand moves across the page more slowly than it types. You are literally slowing yourself down, downshifting from a sprint to a saunter.

Research shows that people are more creative and better at handling complex cognitive concepts when our parasympathetic nervous system is switched on.[3] Rather than being in a reactive, "sympathetic" nervous state, the calmer "parasympathetic" zone is where the muse can often be found. I picture her chilling out in a hammock, hands clasped behind her head, looking up at the sky, patiently waiting for us twitchy humans to relax enough to be communicated with.

Here's a prompt to help you explore your relationship to boredom, cultivating some new awareness, and maybe become a little less antsy, too. Even if your usual mediums for journaling are screen-based, I'd recommend you challenge yourself to do the prompts in this chapter in longhand.

PROMPT: What do you consider boring and why? When was a time that boredom helped you? What creative role/s has boredom played in your life? Consider and write for seven minutes or more.

Humanity has never experienced such an agitating environment, technologically speaking, as the one we're in now. Moore's Law is the accurate prediction made by engineer Gordon Moore in 1975 that the number of transistors per silicon chip would double every two years, resulting in increasingly fast, light, and inexpensive technology.[4] This turned computers from mainframe beasts that filled rooms to the portable machines that we hold in our hands and that are integrated into our cars, appliances, and homes. Our poor brains are constantly playing catch-up, adjusting to all these new interfaces because we take longer to evolve than a semiconductor. We need to give our fried neural circuits a break. An accessible tonic to help you recalibrate is a bit of constructive boredom.

In previous chapters, I've walked you through a whole bunch of creativity prompts that are just a few minutes long to make it easier to integrate mindful writing into a busy schedule. This activity is different by design. It's a large enough container for you to be able to stretch out and get mentally languorous.

PROMPT: Give yourself (at least) twenty uninterrupted minutes to do nothing but journal. Sequester yourself from screens and needy humans. Set a timer, then put your phone in a drawer. Stare out the window, look at the page, write whatever wants to be written. Maybe doodle or sketch, if the urge strikes. If you find yourself getting bored, that's okay. It's kind of the whole point, at least initially. Stay the course, even if it's a bit uncomfortable. You can tap that recognition as a meta-prompt and write about the experience of being bored.

The spigot might flow in fits and spurts, or maybe you will only write a sentence or two. Whatever happens, don't hurry it and don't judge it.

Blasting loud music can be fun in doses, but at prolonged, sustained levels, it's literally used as a form of torture in war zones.[5] Metaphorically, that's what we're doing to ourselves by denying our brains empty space to recover, process, and ideate. Every time you pick up a pen and make the choice to journal with intent for even a few minutes, you're turning down the volume on the pervasive, staticky hum of distraction. Next time your plans go awry, or you're waiting on a platform or queuing up, rather than reaching for a device or swapping in a new plan, invite in a bit of supportive boredom instead. Get acquainted with it, and see what novelty you end up creating out of that space. You probably won't stay bored for long.

21

Stay Curious:

BALLAST, ETHER, AND BREADCRUMBS

There's the practical realm and the innovative realm. Most of us are naturally drawn to one more than the other, but regardless of your natural inclination, we all need to spend some time hanging out in both paradigms to achieve the holy grail of balance. Much like our left and right brain hemispheres, practicality and innovation both play important roles in creativity.

In the practical world, we comb our hair and schedule mammograms. It's not bad; it's prosaic, even necessary. We buy our groceries, pay taxes, and parallel park. The practical world is earthly, providing ballast and grounding. It's where we get stuff done, ticking through to-do lists, making the conceptual visceral.

The innovative world is full of space, of ether. There's room to explore tangents, observe and daydream amidst the unseen, the unknown. It's where imagination takes root and ideas are born. In this realm, plans are hatched, even if we aren't quite sure how it'll all work out. It might not be pragmatic, but it's far from boring.

The treetop clubhouse of innovation can be sublime, but too much time bathing in ether and we might float away (without health insurance or a packed bag). On the other hand, permanent residency in the practical world is a real drag. Devoid of any spontaneity, life turns colorless, monotonous. Journaling is your ally in both realms, and here's a series of conceptual prompts to help you explore each a bit more.

PROMPT: Write or draw what the practical world means to you. How do you function in it? How does it serve you? When you're out of balance, how does the practical world steady you? Conversely, when you're too beholden to the practical, how does it look/feel?

Write or draw your innovative world. Who/what/where helps you feel connected to this realm? What are some of the rituals that help you tap into this space? What does it mean to you? What role does it play in your work/personal life?

Which world do you tend to gravitate toward naturally? How did it feel to write about them both? What did you learn about yourself?

In order to innovate, there has to be enough room to let bits of ideas come to the surface. If our head or day is too full, it becomes harder for those glimmers to snag our attention. Those precious shiny bits are valuable, more so than most of us are taught to believe.

I call my personal creative process "following the breadcrumbs," which has its roots in the tale of Hansel and Gretel. They followed the bits of bread they'd left as clues for themselves to find their way home through the dark forest. They used what was available to them, nothing fancy or contrived. Humble breadcrumbs saved them from peril.

The implication here is that unless you're paying attention, you might miss the cues. Ideas rarely come at you like a bedecked Brazilian samba dancer in full carnival regalia, headdress shaking, hips swinging. "Look at me! I am resplendent!" Sometimes you're that lucky, fireworks and laser lights pointing you THIS WAY. But usually, ideas are more likely to be subtle whispers, like bits of bread on the forest floor.

A few years ago, a magazine invited me to participate in their annual interview issue, giving me free rein to pick anyone I'd been wanting to barrage with questions. I chose the adventurous reporter and author Susan Casey, whose books and articles have been a touchstone for me. In addition to being one hell of a writer, Susan has a lot of moxie.

One of the gemlike quotes from that interview that's stuck with me is a glimpse into Casey's creative process. How curiosity—paying attention to those things that have resonance—is a crucial element of how she works:

"If there's something that haunts you, like if there's a picture of some location, if there's something that you can't get out of your mind, a body of water that calls to you, then I say go there. . . . It's only your own permission that you need to do something like that, so give yourself the permission. If it's an aquatic environment, go swimming in it, go surfing in it, go see it. Go learn more about it, but do go."

We aren't all going to be badass writer-editor-reporters like Casey, and we don't have to be in order to participate in the process. You don't actually need a specific desired outcome at all. Explore for the sake of exploration. Learn for the sake of learning. A nice bonus is that learning is really good for the neuroplasticity of our brains, especially as we age. (Keep that gray matter supple, baby.) See where it takes you, not for any specific outcome or for monetization, but for the enjoyment of following the breadcrumbs.

PROMPT: With Casey's quote as inspiration, what/where/who has piqued your interest lately? It can be a concept, a word, an image, a piece of art, an idea, a place—anything. It doesn't need to make "sense" or be practical in any way. Get quiet and let it float into your field of vision. Make room for it to say hello. What about it is interesting to you?

If you read the above and got nada, nothing, *niente*—don't panic. There's nothing wrong with you. Capturing creative fireflies often takes some practice, especially if you're not used to giving them attention. If you're feeling blocked, here's an alternate subprompt:

It's worth noting on the page if you are having trouble coming up with anything that's been nudging you recently. Why do you think that is? When was the last time you did take note of a potential breadcrumb? Did you follow up on it? If so, how did it go? If not, what held you back? By identifying patterns, you're unclogging your own creative machinery.

Now that something you're curious about has landed in your awareness, what incremental, practical steps can you take to further explore what's tugging your sleeve? How can you spend more time with it/in it/on it? What resources can you dedicate to it? Who can help? You don't need to map the entire plan here, now, but begin considering it on the page. What are the first three tangible steps you can take, and when will you do them?

What I've witnessed repeatedly in my experience as a creative coach is that, when my brave and wise clients free themselves up to explore a subject that speaks to them, without any expectation of expertise or an attachment to productivity, a really useful outcome tends to emerge. A new business model comes into focus; a different way of seeing their work is revealed; a creative project suddenly takes shape. Transformation occurs. It probably didn't happen in a straight line, but suddenly: There it is.

In addition to giving myself the freedom to imagine, my own creative journey has taken a lot of careful planning and commitment along the way. No magic wands here. To take an idea and make it material, we need boots on the ground, to invest our time. One of my favorite examples of this is something the celebrated American artist Jeff Koons purportedly said to a journalist. Koons is best known for his large-scale whimsical sculptures depicting modern iconography, such as balloon animals, installing them in high-traffic public spaces, including Rockefeller Center. When asked what tool he used most frequently to create art, he replied, "The telephone." It wasn't a polymer, epoxy, pencil lead, or steel. A phone allowed him to network, manage red tape, organize, publicize, galvanize support, and fundraise. Communication enables Koons to actualize his artistic vision. That's wild innovation married to clear-eyed practicality. Which is how and why you are reading this book. It's a collaboration between the two of us. Your curiosity led you here to this page, to this sentence, on this day. Something about it called your name—"Pssst, this way." And the book exists because I followed a similar series of impulses. I had an idea, I created a single blank notebook, and then a curriculum, and then a series of workshops all because I respected the glimmers enough to listen to them (in the innovative world) and to then act on them (in the practical world). I didn't expect it to lead here, but I'm so glad we landed in this place together.

PART 3

Having a Blast:

Launching Personal Rocket Ships

"Good enough" isn't what this section is about. We are priming you for greatness—however you define it. Welcome to Part 3, helping you mindfully write your way to clear-eyed wisdom and joy. Meet a happier, more present, and creatively expressed version of yourself on the page. Here you'll learn how to avoid common pitfalls and give yourself permission to pursue your dreamiest dreams.

It's all happening now. We are on our way to full bloom. Here. We. Go!

22

The Grateful Head:

UP-LEVEL YOUR GRATITUDE PRACTICE

Some lucky humans are just naturally happy. Their brain chemistry is favorable, their glass of cabernet is half full. While that sounds nice, I wasn't built that way. My innate baseline setting hovers somewhere between on-high-alert and mildly concerned. But through consistent cultivation, I've been able to shift my mood for the better. It turns out that one of the most effective ways to chill out and cheer up is to repeatedly focus on what you appreciate. Anxiety is a future-focused worry—what may or may not happen. Gratitude disrupts that pattern; over time, it provides a brighter lens.[1] "Well, isn't this rad?" instead of "Everything's about to go to hell."

A note on anxiety. It's not all bad. Heck, it's served me really well from time to time, particularly in professional settings. I could see a potential pothole, a zig and a zag looming, and I'd already planned for it. Scanning for threats is an evolutionary tool and not one I'm relegating to the dustbin.[2] It has its uses; I just don't want it to be the primary lens through which I experience life because that would be a tragic waste. Gratitude has given me a different pair of glasses, but rather than being rose-tinted, they are reflective and clear.

Being thankful shouldn't be reserved just for momentous moments and red-letter days, like the birth of a niece, a milestone, a birthday, or the day you score a dreamy gig. Wonderful days are just that. Wonderful. But hoarding our appreciation just for the ALL CAPS occasions means we're missing out. We do a lot of living in between those events, and that terrain is worthy of gratitude, too. There's plenty of good happening in the day-to-day, though recognizing it takes practice for some of us.

With consistency, seeing the bright(er) side becomes a reflex. Gratitude can help you retrain your brain via "the Tetris effect."[3] Via extended, repetitive play, the OG video game of interlocking, stacking geometric shapes has been known to have an impact on people's brains, potentially enhancing a person's memory while increasing motor and cognitive development.[4] Similarly, the effect of repeating and retaining a more positive thinking pattern has powerful and proven upsides. Over the past two decades, studies have consistently found that people who focus on gratitude report fewer symptoms of illness,[5] more optimism and happiness,[6] stronger relationships,[7] better heart health, improved sleep,[8] and more generous behavior. You become a healthier and happier person.

Writing down what you appreciate will begin to feel good, especially once you get the hang of it. And, look, I know that gratitude lists can end up sounding kinda corny. "I am grateful for the sun. I am grateful for the moon." It can all be a bit . . . dream catchers and prayer flags. Personally, not my thing. Hold the patchouli. Instead, here are some pen-to-paper exercises to get you started, and keep your practice fresh and inspiring.

PROMPT:

- Scan your life—go macro and micro. Mine for grace in the big picture, and look for it in the smallest gestures and moments.

- Tap into your senses. What sights, sounds, tastes, textures, and scents are you grateful for?

- Don't stop at the "what" in what makes you happy. Go further, tap into the *why*. Why are you grateful for the items on your list? There are gems of awareness waiting for you here.

- Switch up the language lens, do a love scan. List all the big and small ways love showed up for you today. It's particularly rewarding to do this exercise at the end of the day, as a way to wind down and reflect.

And please, ditch the gratitude guilt. Workshop participants have shared that they sometimes feel rotten if they don't write down everything they think is supposed to go on their list. As if by not writing down how much they appreciate Grandma's health, they're in some way putting a hex on Grandma. Bummer associations like these only create impediments between you and your journal. Granny certainly wouldn't want that. So, if you find that dynamic creeping in, here's a hack to try out.

PROMPT: If you find your practice gets repetitive over time, create an entry of your "usual suspects" and park them on the page. Voilà! You are officially grateful for these things in perpetuity. Now look further afield, and scan your life for additional things for which to be grateful.

You're on a roll. Okay, what's next? I find that writing down everything that is right in my world started to feel limited and a bit selfish. I wanted others to get the benefits of my practice, to share in the upside. So I created a prompt-activity hybrid that I call "Gratitude with Feet." Why feet? Because it walks right out your door and into the world.

PROMPT: Via whatever means, write a simple note of thanks to someone who has positively impacted you and your life. Not for anything transactional, like a present or a bonus. This isn't a thank-you card to Aunt Irene for the birthday bucks. Identify a simple act of kindness, a moment that mattered, a way of being that shed light in the dark—these are the subtle but important things that might otherwise go unsaid, unhonored.

This doesn't have to be an exhaustive letter; no need to get bogged down. A few sentences will do, and off it goes. And just wait to see what comes back your way. It tends to be pretty wonderful.

As a way of encouraging analog communication, I collect postcards on my travels. Some are nostalgic or edgy; others are aspirational or a little weird. A stop at Graceland offered a particularly good haul—Elvis's recipe for a peanut butter, banana, and bacon sandwich. I use these postcards to send notes to people I care about, but I also gather them for a writing activity in which I invite participants to engage with the "Gratitude with Feet" prompt. During this part of a workshop, I pass around trays of these postcards, letting participants choose whatever image best suits their particular message and recipient. Everyone fills one out. Postworkshop, I stamp and send these emissaries off via snail mail, creating a wave of gratitude.

What began to happen next initially surprised me. I started getting feedback from participants. They shared how much the postcard had meant to the recipient, how it opened up conversations, deepened bonds, and created meaning for both the writer and receiver. The admiration and appreciation ricocheted right back to them. All from a humble postcard, a few thoughtful words, and a stamp—peanut butter, banana, and bacon sandwiches notwithstanding.

23

The Wellness Trap:

PRAISE BE

Generally speaking, our culture is stingy with praise. I've heard people say they wish they could hear their eulogy while they were still alive, probably because we could all use a round of applause from the people who love us most. Well, the person who loves you most should be *you*. As scary or uncomfortable a concept as that may be, it's fundamentally true. Fostering self-love requires zero commerce, though the health and wellness industry is happy to sell you a multitude of products to address a nagging sense of not being enough.

"We can fix you." That's the overarching promise of the wellness business, that if you invest in X and/or Y, you will become a better, improved version of yourself. It's important to understand that this massive industry—$6.3 trillion globally as of 2024—is predicated on selling you self-improvement solutions.[1] Supplements, mats, gear, trips, outfits, things to slather on, bathe in, inject, drink down, breathe, and listen to. You name it, there's a scented candle for it. Subtly or explicitly, this implies you need fixing, rather than celebrating the wondrous, beautiful human you already are.

Beyond all the self-care sector's carrot-on-a-stick commotion is something invaluable, and it doesn't require spending a single cent. It's owning your own worth *as you are*, not wishing for some other, more magical version of yourself. You are plenty magical right now in this very moment, in this exact form. Those eyes. That smile. Each breath in and out of your body. You are nothing short of a miracle of complex physical and energetic systems (respiration, elimination, regeneration, and, wow, many more) working in astonishingly detailed cooperation to support you. Given all that, spending some time appreciating yourself just feels like good manners.

Nonetheless, humans naturally prioritize criticism over praise.[2] We tend to dwell on and remember perceived disapproval versus compliments. Add to that our natural inclination to deflect rather than absorb positive feedback, and it's a wonder anyone ever feels good about themselves.[3] We're fighting against the tide just to stay level. In order to increase self-respect, we need to game the system. Here's one effective way, using pen and paper.

PROMPT: Start a self-appreciation list. Write down ten things you like and appreciate about yourself. For bonus points, go for twenty.

This is a gratitude list of sorts, but here you are expressing gratitude for your own damn self. Call things out. Sing your own praises. We're not seeking out perfection; perfectionism is cruel and not to be trusted.

Maybe you make a great grilled-cheese sandwich or you're a good listener. Traits, actions, habits—claim them all. For instance, I don't take my phone with me when I walk my dog. I want to be attentive to her, so I ditch mobile devices when I grab the leash. I like that about myself. And I have lovely wrists, slim and elegant. I'm also not a flaky person. If I say I'm going to do something, my friends can count on me to do it. These are a few things I recently discovered and wrote down. I wasn't explicitly aware of these characteristics until they showed up on the page.

If you're struggling with the exercise, try turning it inside out. Think of someone that loves you who makes you feel safe, then draft the list from their perspective. (Get creative. It can even be your pet.) What elements would they call out in appreciation? You can skip around, adding items from your most-trustworthy people, until you're able to self-select some attributes that you think are pretty cool about yourself, too.

Take a beat to reread your list and reflect on the exercise. How did it feel? What did you learn? Was it harder or easier than you expected? The more difficult this is for you, the more you need (and will gain) from it.

This isn't one and done. On an ongoing basis, continue to add to your list. By regularly engaging in this practice, and challenging yourself to do it frequently, you are shifting your default neural pathways, becoming increasingly self-positive. It's okay if this feels awkward, but it's actually good for you. A sense of well-being and optimism can help insulate us from the stress of extreme situations.[4] Your sense of worthiness becomes a valuable shield when you need it most.

To keep the prompt fresh, explore different categories. You can ask yourself where you need a jolt of TLC and focus your admiration accordingly. As an example, one of my creative-coaching clients was confident in her professional accomplishments and management abilities, but on the personal front, she needed some positive reinforcement as a partner, mother, and woman. So we pivoted the activity and had her forgo adding any workplace-related elements to her list. It was tougher for her initially, but also a lot more rewarding. She got the particular boost she needed, and so can you.

Sure, light the candle, treat yourself to a new pair of Pilates socks, and take your liposomal vitamins. But do it from a place of celebrated wholeness, and you're transforming the act. Instead of trying to fix broken bits or chasing trends, you're cherishing all the amazingness that is you. And that, right there, is some real-deal, genuine wellness.

24

Group Swim:

WHEN JOURNALING IS BETTER TOGETHER

Although I'm not unathletic, I've never really been into team sports. The possibility of letting someone down feels like way too much pressure for it to be fun. Surfing, hiking, yoga, tennis, count me in. Need one more player for your softball league? I'm definitely busy that afternoon.

Similarly, by its nature, journaling is a solo activity. It's just you and the page, an analog, private pursuit. Yet I've witnessed something repeatedly occur while leading hundreds of mindful writing workshops, where groups of people are journaling separately *together*. A certain X-factor seems to enter the room; it happens even in digital "rooms." Each time I lead a session, I feel it click into a place where a kind of collective mind coalesces.[1] It's a beautiful thing to witness, and it usually happens while participants aren't even speaking. Pens moving, present and focused, a group flow state emerges.

I can't take all the credit here. Sure, I'm confident in my craft as a skilled facilitator, but this dynamic is the sum of multiple parts. I'm only one factor in the mix.

Much like parallel play,[2] where children play independently alongside one another, workshop participants are drawing on the supportive energy of being in community—all without the pressure to constantly engage. Even while not interacting with one another, focusing instead on individual reflection and personal creativity, they're still being valuably influenced by the group. It's soothing and inspiring to share a common experience, especially if journaling might otherwise feel awkward or a bit intimidating. Instead, you have behavior modeled on either side. "Well, if she can do it, so can I." Heck yes, you can.

Group participants are also more likely to deepen and maintain focus for longer periods of time. For the duration of the workshop, we communally agree to mute outside distractions—yielding greater concentration, enhanced critical thinking, and more creative room to roam.[3] Plus it's fun, but you don't need to attend one of my mindful writing experiences to derive the benefits. Take the parallel-play approach to journaling for a test drive.

PROMPT: Make a date to journal with a friend (or gather multiple friends). You can meet up at a café, at the beach, or your kitchen table, or even make it a digital meetup. Maybe each of you brings a prompt for the group to take for a spin, or you pick an overarching theme, or everyone just quietly does their own thing. Sort of like a gym buddy, but for journaling.

Some best-practice recommendations:

- Mutually commit to the amount of time up front, whatever it may be (twenty minutes, etc.).
- Silence or turn off mobile devices to limit tempting interruptions.
- You don't need to share what you've written. The point here is the tacit support you're providing each other to invoke flow state. It's therapeutic but not therapy.
- Wrap up with a check-in. How did it go? What could you add or change to improve the experience for yourself and each other? Give each participant (including yourself) a minute or more to share, as needed.

Life gets busy, so if timing doesn't sync up or you're geographically challenged, there are other ways to give and receive support. Even if you aren't gathering in real time, you can create your own virtual cohort.

PROMPT: Pick your people. It can be some long-distance friends, or even a romantic partner. Either way, a shared commitment helps you stay accountable and a little more dedicated. You can mutually try the same approach (such as 4 x 4 x 4), but you don't need to. Here are some helpful tips:

- You can each choose your own amount of time/number of days per week that you'll be journaling. Whatever works for you individually.
- Write down that commitment and tell each other what it is. This helps you stick with your own program.

- Do periodic check-ins, every week or so. A group text or email works. Keep it casual. "Hello, journaling all-stars. How are we doing?"

- No need to be dogmatic. Every so often, you can update your commitment based on what could make your own journaling experience more enjoyable or interesting. Maybe you want to explore a different theme or prompt style. Switch it up. And please, no need to police each other. Park the journaling guilt elsewhere. This is about support, not being punitive. Bossy vibes are not a value-add.

You're still essentially journaling solo, but you're not alone. Either approach is a way for you to receive and offer support for your pen-to-paper practice. Dive in, and see where it takes you. Go, team.

25

Coupled Up:

JOURNALING INTO PARTNERSHIP

When it comes to romance, mindful writing can be like taking your "love vitamins," strengthening your system for a more robust and healthier outcome. Often, we associate journaling with heartrending ruptures, things going awfully, terribly wrong. It can also help things go delightfully, satisfyingly right at multiple stages of a romantic relationship—from first dates to silver anniversaries.

When you're seeking meaningful partnership, there can be an underlying "pick me!" energy to dating. That hopefulness often creates blind spots, making it harder to see the other person as they truly are. In the throes of infatuation, we become more susceptible to ignoring red flags and sometimes overlooking green flags, too.[1] Once you're aware of the attributes you're looking for in a partner, you're more likely to recognize a great mate when they come along. Writing down those elements isn't spell-casting manifestation; you're bringing the unconscious into conscious awareness.

PROMPT: Do you know what your "green flags" in a partner consist of? Not just the material, visceral aspects, such as what they look like or do for a living. Those things can change drastically (over time or in a swift blow) and don't tend to be strong foundational elements on which to build partnership. Character traits, communication styles, their approach to life, faith, and partnership—those are more enduring values and characteristics. For instance, follow-through is a big one for me. Doing what you say you'll do isn't just attractive, it's important. Patience is another green flag of mine, as is the willingness to try new things, to keep learning. Take some time to consider what your green flags are and write them down on the page.

While this chapter is focused on romantic explorations, this exercise works well for other kinds of partnership, too. As an example, if you're looking to go into business with someone or take on an investor, it's empowering to determine on the front end what foundational elements you're looking for. You'll know them when you meet them and be less apt to get distracted by the size of their wallet.

Back to cupid. When you're single, you have the incredible opportunity to choose your partner, not just be chosen. But, hey, it can be hard to be discerning when they're hot. Here's a postdate exercise to help you cultivate dating acuity when you're getting to know someone, even amidst a hormonal haze.

PROMPT: Got (phenylethylamine-fueled) butterflies in your stomach?[2] Let's give them a place to land. We often get so caught up in whether the shiny-object person likes us, we can forget that discernment here is mutual. After spending time with this potential mate, do a check-in on the page. Some questions to help:

- How do you feel mentally, physically, emotionally? Are you buoyant, grounded, exhilarated, uneasy, exhausted?
- What kinds of questions did they ask you? Did they listen to your answers and respond?
- How do they treat the people around them?
- What are five adjectives that describe their personality?

Take time to consider your experience and practice your powers of discernment.

If you're already in a partnership, mindful writing is a potent tool for maintaining (and increasing) the quality of your coupledom. Emotional intelligence (the ability to perceive, understand, and regulate your emotions) is a key factor in relationship satisfaction,[3] and a great way to develop that is, no surprise, by keeping a journal. The time you dedicate to your pen-to-paper practice isn't self-obsessed indulgence. It's beneficial to both of you.

One interesting study on the topic took newly dating duos and had one person in each couple journal their deepest emotions and feelings about the young relationship for three consecutive days.[4] The control group wrote about their daily activities, unrelated to romance. Months later, the participants who'd spent time mindfully writing about their relationship were significantly more likely to still be dating the same partner. The practice helped the nascent bond both endure and become more positive. Notably, these favorable outcomes were created by only one person in the relationship journaling. While I can't state this empirically, it does imply that if both partners were journaling, the results could be exponentially favorable. After all, two oars in the water are better than one.

Realistically, any enduring relationship hits some rough patches along the way. Take it from my personal experience, starting a conversation with righteous indignation doesn't usually result in a fruitful discourse. So, instead, when I get all worked up over something, I take it to the page where I can discharge some energy. I find that by writing out my emotions, I gain new perspective. When I subsequently bring the concern to my partner, instead of doing my best screech-owl impression, my approach is more constructive.

Sometimes after a writing session, I realize whatever was irking me isn't actually that important after all. What felt like a scalding "nine" is really more like a lukewarm-ish "three and a half." Journal-fueled discernment—determining what's worth leaning into and what you can let go of—is helpful in any kind of interpersonal relationship, romantic and otherwise.

Taking time to appreciate your partner on the page shouldn't be relegated to the space in a Valentine's Day card. How to keep the flame of ardor burning? When you journal about what's good about your relationship, it can have ripple effects. Do the opposite of nitpicking, and write down things you appreciate, admire, and find attractive about your partner. Stoke the flames of idealization a bit; put the stars back in your eyes. Doing so renders you more prescient than blind, better able to quiet doubts and navigate conflicts over time.[5] Wave those green flags on the page, and you're more likely to stay happily coupled up.

26

Bye-Bye, Blocks:

BRICK BY BRICK

Being creatively immobilized can feel lonely, but you're actually in excellent company. From Leo Tolstoy to Maya Angelou, some of the finest writers to ever string words together have suffered similarly. It's a surprisingly common dynamic, even for the greats. So really, it's not just you.

I've had clients reach out, frustrated and blocked, sitting at their computers, nearly in tears. They can't make any headway on the task in front of them and don't know where to go or what to do. That's when I usually suggest they downshift. Here's my Rx to help break through:

- Entrenched and can't make any headway? Don't just sit there, bathing in frustration. This is a great time to walk away from your desk—and keep going. Literally step outside and take a walk for at least twenty minutes.[1] It's been proven to provide a creative boost.[2] Many celebrated writers (Charles Dickens, Haruki Murakami, Zadie Smith, and many more) cite going for walks as an essential part of their creative process. If it's good enough for Wordsworth, it's certainly good enough for me.

- Slip into "soft fascination" mode, otherwise known as Attention Recovery Therapy (ART).[3] Do something diverting but not draining to help your brain rest and recover.[4] This also provides some space for creativity to tiptoe back in through the side door. Take a shower, fold laundry, mow the lawn, go for a drive, water your plants, anything that engages but doesn't overtax your mind.[5] Bonus points if you can interact with the natural world in some way.[6] Even arranging flowers or looking at clouds can help get you there.

- After taking these steps, if you still feel stuck, don't return to the computer. Instead, open a notebook. Write something, write anything. It can be banal song lyrics you know by heart or what you had for breakfast. You can draw, doodle. It's less about what you do than the act of doing it, starting to wade back into the creative stream.

Between moving your body, resetting your focus , and putting pen to paper, you're getting loosened up in low-stakes environments, like shadowboxing outside the ring.

Still blocked and locked? Here's a prompt to help get your task-related creativity flowing again by naming and removing barriers. Creative blocks are made of fear. They're not real in 3D, but those walls can feel impenetrable when you're pressed up against them. Let's dissect that wall, one brick at a time, by journaling about what it is you're actually afraid of.

PROMPT: Draw out a wall of big boxes or "bricks," and write a task-related fear in each one of them. Jot down what's holding you back, such as, "I'm afraid of being found out that I'm not actually talented." In the next, write another fear: "Disappointing my subject, not doing her justice." And so on until your fear-well runs dry. Once you can see the niggling thoughts that are actually holding you back, they aren't usually as weighty. The death grip loosens.

Next, deconstruct those bricks. Blow them up by writing down at least one correlating fact that counters your fear. For instance, my coaching client wouldn't have been assigned the feature story if they weren't talented to begin with, and they have a large existing body of work that demonstrates it. And their subject is hugely stoked to be written about at all, especially in such a prestigious outlet.

As you go through this process, cross out your fears, one by one. Ciao! Sayonara! And when you're done, read through the substantiating facts of why this, why you, why now. Say them out loud.

The combination of all of the above usually works wonders, picking the perceived locks, getting my clients back on track. I recommend trying them out and seeing which suit your needs. Sometimes it takes a jump start to get back in the zone, but the very first step is to stop blaming yourself. That only entrenches the immobility. Enough with the masochism! Consider your block a badge of honor, a rite of passage, one you wouldn't achieve if you weren't trying to make something from nothing, a process that requires courage. So, let's channel that mojo into a more generative mind-set, add some intellectual curiosity to the mix, and learn something new: What helps you become less blocked? Go find out. Take it for a walk. Name it. Make friends with whatever's holding you back, and watch it shrink, brick by brick.

27

Permission Slips:

BACK-TO-SCHOOL SEASON (FOR YOUR BRAIN)

While I am undeniably devoted to summer, every fall I get nostalgic for reams of three-ring binder paper and black-and-white marbled composition books. To paraphrase Nora Ephron, there's something about that time of year that makes me want to buy school supplies. Putting summer fun behind me, I'm ready to shake the sand out of my hair and go learn something.

Growing up, back to school meant "New teachers! New classes! New classmates!"—all the unknowns (with their attendant combo of excitement and stressors). Everything's possible—it's a clean slate. In adulthood, we don't have as many of these distinct and defined new beginnings. Sure, there's New Year's Day, but, practically speaking, on January 1 nothing really changes except the calendar. If you're feeling stuck in a bit of a rut, you can opt in for a fresh start any old time. No need to climb aboard a yellow bus. Instead, let's channel some sense of possibility with a writing exercise.

PROMPT:

PART 1. What does the phrase "fresh start" mean to you? Where does that feeling arise in your adult life? Try out writing your answer for at least five full minutes. The essence of the challenge here is to do this without it feeling like:

- It's a test.
- Someone will be grading you.
- You're going to have to read it aloud in front of the class.

Because none of the above is true. Unlike a pop quiz, your journal is for one set of eyes only—*your own*. Dare yourself to be fully, wildly uncensored for five full minutes.

PART 2. After you write, check in with yourself. Maybe reread what you've written. What imagery showed up? What emotions emerged? Was it fraught, exhilarating? Both? Try to be aware of your reactions without judging them; then come back to the page to sift through your experience.

Continuing our education isn't just interesting; it's good for our brains. Being open to learning new things (particularly complex ones) is a great way to boost neuroplasticity, and even make new neurons—a process known as "neurogenesis"[1]—which enables us to keep learning new stuff.[2] It used to be believed that, after childhood, it was all downhill in the neurogenesis department, but newer research has revealed that our noggins never stop changing in response to learning.[3] Even grown-ups can score new neurons, as long as you're engaging in the right activities. The result is lowered risk of Alzheimer's,[4] improved memory recall, and slowing down age-related cognitive decline.[5]

Here's a neuroplasticity cheat sheet, delineating some effective ways to stay mentally limber:

Neuroplasticity Cheat Sheet

- Explore new places, travel; even local explorations help fire up neurogenesis.[6]
- Seek out novelty: try a new way home, a different restaurant or exercise class.[7]
- Read more,[8] especially fiction.[9]
- Learn something complex (a language,[10] music,[11] etc.).
- Be creative; make stuff.[12]
- Exercise regularly.[13]
- Get plenty of rest.[14]

- Hit the dance floor.[15]

- Get enough vitamin D[16] and magnesium.[17]

- Take naps[18] (twenty minutes in the afternoon is ideal).

- Expand your vocabulary; learn some new words.

- Try writing or drawing with your nondominant hand.[19]

Since I've asked you to revisit back-to-school season, let's build on that theme with a prompt that incorporates pathways to neuroplasticity.

PROMPT: Write yourself a permission slip for that thing you have been wanting to do. What is it? What subject, skill, or experience do you find intriguing but haven't prioritized the time and attention to explore? Invite in a spirit of irreverence, a lack of constraints. What have you been itching to do, but you thought it was extravagant, unproductive, or kinda random? We live so much of our lives waiting to act on our desires and dreams, when often the only consent we really need is our own.

Give yourself a green light on the page. Choose the where and the when, include some helpful resources. Here's an example from my own life. I'm self-employed, so I wrote my "boss" a note:

> *Dear Boss,*
>
> *Laura cannot come to work next Wednesday because she needs to go rock climbing. She's been afraid of heights her whole life and wants to finally conquer it. So she's going to get herself some lessons and go to Malibu Creek*

State Park with an instructor—and a friend for moral support.

Thank you for your understanding.

Sincerely,
Me

Or whatever! It should only take a few minutes. Permission slips aren't lengthy. No need to make excuses here; you won't end up sitting in detention.

In both of the above prompts, we're ushering in a beginner's mindset, one of the essential pathways to creativity. Adults don't typically give themselves many opportunities to say, "I don't know how to do this, but I want to try," particularly without being attached to the outcome. Over time, this is detrimental to both risk-taking and neurogenesis, leaching life of its novelty as well as aiding cognitive decline.

So, let's keep learning. Continuing to explore what interests us (no advanced calculus for me, thank you very much) helps our brains stay limber and healthy. It's "Take Your Neurons to School Day," and class is in session.

28

Slow Your Roll:

THE ART OF DECELERATING

Longhand, the act of pen on paper, can be frustrating. We've become accustomed to the speed of a keyboard, but putting away devices occasionally means our over-stimulated noggins get a chance to process information differently.[1] Our neural activity changes, resting the brain and increasing creativity.[2] Slow and smart is your brain on longhand.

In general, operating slowly has fallen out of favor in our e-commerce-driven, "more, now" culture of immediacy. Speed implies efficiency, novelty, decisiveness, whereas slow service connotes laziness. And if someone is described as "slow," it implies they're not exactly the brightest bulb.

Take a moment to explore your own relationship with decelerating via what I call a Writing Rorschach, inspired by the inkblot tests of the 1900s. In these studies, subjects were shown abstract images and asked to describe them, thereby revealing aspects of the subject's personality.[3] There weren't right or wrong answers, just information. Similarly, the essence of the prompt below is about accessing your first and unfiltered response.

PROMPT: When you hear/read the word "slow," what do you immediately think of? What connotations does it have? What words float into your mind? What images or sensations come up? Don't overthink your response, and definitely don't judge it. Write continuously for four minutes or more.

Once you've completed that step, reread what you've written. This exercise is designed to help tap into your own biases and preferences without too much extraneous opinion muddying the waters. Did anything surprise you? Do you feel any shift in your body? Did it soothe you to write about slowness, or did it perhaps make you anxious and uncomfortable?

Motivated by my tendency to overschedule myself (and therefore run slightly late), I challenged myself to not rush for an entire month—physically and intellectually. Aspiring to feel European, I chose August. Granted, I couldn't take the month off work, but thirty-one days of moving through my life more slowly and intentionally, and being more considered in my thought processes, sounded great. In execution, it was harder than expected. I still tended to show up at yoga just before class started rather than being one of those virtuous people serenely lolling on their mats with loads of time to spare. But I wasn't the last student to arrive anymore, either. Which was an improvement, because "yoga stress" is counterproductive.

The aspect of my monthlong experiment I came to appreciate most wasn't the extra bits of time I bubble wrapped around events in my calendar. It was recognizing—and sloughing off—the cultural pressure to have an instantly formed opinion on almost everything the news cycle throws our way. There's an enormous amount of personal power in saying, "I don't know yet," rather than committing to a perspective that isn't fully baked.

When you're not hurrying intellectually, there's more time between points A and B, literally and otherwise. Being in liminal spaces, hanging out in the in-between, can be uncomfortable because it's not defined. But there's also abundant creative potential and freedom in it. Watching events unfold, evaluating data, and maybe only then forming an opinion—versus rushing to a conclusion—that's where wisdom accumulates.

Utilizing this perspective, here's a chance for you to rewrite the script of an event from your past, to have a Redux Reflection.

PROMPT: When in life would it have benefited you to go more slowly, to move more deliberately—physically or mentally? Pick an instance. You are giving yourself the opportunity to rewrite that scenario. How might it have looked if you had slowed yourself down? Maybe you didn't jump to that misinformed conclusion, or you wouldn't have been pulled over for a speeding ticket? You can evaluate and rescript the scene.

This isn't about regret or self-blame; it's a reclamation of an experience. In your journal, you get a do-over. If this rescripting approach is uncomfortable, you can simply explore why you think slowing down might have helped.

Put the timer away for this one. Let it take the time it takes.

Going slowly allows us to pay closer attention. Not just to the microdetails ("stop and smell the roses"), but also to zoom out and regard occurrences as part of a bigger picture. Observing events with more information results in fewer errors.

We've established that slow is smart, but it's also sexy.[4] Moving at your own pace telegraphs confidence and, rather hedonistically, helps us savor what's in front of us.

With the evidence stacking up, how do you want to incorporate this lower gear into your present and future? Here's a mindful journaling prompt to help.

PROMPT: Where would it benefit you (and by extension, your community) to slow down—mentally, emotionally, physically, etc.? What adjustments can you make to support bringing more deliberate slowness into your life?

- Immediate: today/tomorrow

- Short-term: this week/month

- Longer-term: the upcoming quarter/six months, next year, and beyond

Need a nudge to get going? Here are some examples:

- Try chewing more slowly to derive more pleasure from your food (and get full sooner).[5]

- Schedule brief nature breaks every day to help reduce the drain of task-switching.[6]

- Get more organized so you know where your keys/glasses/ phone are every time you leave the house, reducing those frantic minutes on your way out the door. You'll be less apt to speed and will drive more safely for everyone on the road.

- Step away from your devices for at least an hour before you respond to an irksome message, reducing interpersonal friction.

- Try out saying, "I don't know what I think about that yet," rather than cobbling together an opinion or re-purposing someone else's perspective.

- Create a "slow word" trigger that represents a de-escalation, one you can say to yourself (and maybe you and your partner or friends can say to each other) when you feel that careening sensation start to creep in.

- Try taking notes and making lists by hand rather than on devices; experiment with how/if that changes the ways you interpret, integrate, and retain information.

Again, there is no time limit on this prompt. Stretch out, get creative, enjoy having the space to ideate, and imagine a different way forward.

Keyboards aren't the enemy, and cursive script isn't the point here. I'm certainly not buying a quill anytime soon. Decelerating is a mind shift, allowing us to operate with more clarity and intention. In an age that's encouraging us to go faster and consume more—to believe that quarter-over-quarter earnings and shareholder value are what matter most *above all else*—slowing down and being our authentic selves is a significant counterculture accomplishment.

29

Don't Quit Before the Miracle:

EVADING THE VACUUM

Despite profound "lightbulb" moments, I find that lasting, integrated changes don't usually occur in a flash. They need some time (and commitment) to take root, and that process often brings with it a stretch of uncomfortable, wobbly territory. You've left one shore, but you haven't quite arrived at the next one. Case in point: I was speaking with a client who'd made an impressive leap—away from her established professional direction as an academic and toward a fresh, exciting new chapter as a working creative. But she was languishing in what I call The Vacuum, where dreams can stall out. What it takes to push through this discouraging trap can feel counterintuitive. To help you steer, let's sequentially travel through The Vacuum's undermining dynamic:

1. There's the "before." You've decided that your current state is no longer a fit. You're ready to move on toward what resonates—personally, creatively, professionally, all of the above, whatever.

2. You have a vision for where you're going. Congratulations! This is good. You're pretty amped, and you dive into execution mode.

3. You've generated a bit of traction but not enough to fully validate your decision. Maybe the money hasn't started flowing yet, or the viewership of your YouTube series is still largely made up of people who know you ("Hi, Mom!"), or you've realized that you're going to need a lot more help or training or resources than you anticipated to get this project operating at full tilt.

4. Instead of recognizing incremental wins or calling in more support, you start to question your judgment. Why am I doing this crazy thing?

5. Cue the freefall. Welcome to The Vacuum, in which you're drinking down a strong cocktail of self-doubt and panic. Right about now, the perceived safety of the old paradigm starts to look pretty good.

This is the critical moment of inflection. Not (1) when you made the choice, or (2) crafted the vision. Those are important, but frankly, they're comparatively easy. No, The Vacuum is where doubt wants to take the wheel—and put you in park. Alternatively, staying the course requires some grit and grace.

Guitarist George Harrison and his wife, Olivia, had been married for twenty-three years when he passed away, a substantial feat for any couple but particularly impressive in the context of rock n' roll relationships. In an interview, the Beatle's widow was asked about the secret to a long marriage.[1] Olivia Harrison's advice was simple, sage, and highly applicable here: "You don't get divorced." Similarly, when people ask me how I've managed to be self-employed for over twenty years (during which time I've founded two companies and pivoted my ass off), the answer is also really straightforward, "You just keep going." I've come to see entrepreneurialism as one of my creative outlets, in which my self-sustaining mantra is, "Don't quit before the miracle." There have been so many junctures at which I've been tempted to give up or give in, wishing I'd picked an "easier" mission (when in truth, it really picked me). Instead, I've repeated that touchstone phrase and stayed the course because I truly believe in the necessity and power of bringing people to the page, of putting a pen in *your* hand.

Miraculous moments do occur, springboards that propel you forward, but you also need to be open to receiving them. In the case of the talented coaching client I described above, a multinational luxury hospitality group requested a proposal from her for a floor-to-ceiling permanent art installation. When I complimented her on the news, she demurred. It wasn't *real* yet to her. Not until the proposal had been accepted and her art was on the walls; that's when the opportunity would matter. But she was missing out on a valuable data point.

Regardless of the outcome, the inquiry was an important piece of market input, not something to be minimized or skipped over. Whether or not this particular gig happened, it indicated that she was clearly headed in the right direction. Her work was resonating with decision-makers at a high level. I asked her, "If I had told you four months ago that this company would be contacting you for a commission on this scale, would you have believed me?" No. Not a chance. With her "Vacuum goggles" on, she wasn't seeing that the market was already giving her helpful, affirming feedback. And it was telling her: Just. Keep. Going. (BTW, she did end up scoring the gig.)

If you do keep going, eventually you'll make it to a new destination. It might not be exactly the one you expected, but you'll be enriched by the experience. And it's sure to be a lot more interesting than opting out of the adventure. In the meantime, try to celebrate incremental wins and find joy in the process.

The same is true of your journaling practice. Whether you've been diligent in putting pen to paper but haven't yet experienced the full range of benefits you expected, or you're having a tough time sticking with it at all, this is when it's important to not jump ship. Don't abandon your notebook on a shelf, letting The Vacuum claim another victory. Instead, scan your experience for some triumphs, and be emboldened by them. Maybe there was an instance when you committed to writing for only four minutes, but you wrote for five or six. Or a moment when you became aware of the bossy, critical voice in your head, but rather than shutting down, you told it to hush up and kept writing instead.

In truth, each and every time you show up for yourself and put words on paper, it's a win. So here's a prompt inspired by this chapter to bring you back to your practice. Simply by taking it for a spin, you're hitting a kind of inflection point in your creative process. You aren't quitting—no, sir. On the contrary, you're making space for miracles.

PROMPT: Consider on the page, what have been some inflection points in your own life? Where were you nudged forward, past the dreaded Vacuum, and gently (or not so gently) given a course correction? At the time, you may have thought these occurrences were incidental, but looking back, you can now see how pivotal they were and maybe continue to be. Write for ten minutes or more, identifying three different (big or small) moments when this dynamic touched your life and how they changed you and your trajectory.

PART 4

Digging In:

When Times Get Tough

"Break glass in case of emergency." When navigating troubled times, you don't have to do it alone—or blindly. Your notebook is your ally. Here's a tool kit to help you process (and grow from) real-world difficulties.

The biggest "locks" offer the richest opportunities for personal development and insight. Even if they come packaged like gnarly bank vaults. This, the most deeply personal and vulnerable section of the book, includes heartbreak, stories of redemption, and big truths. Let's dig in and go there together.

30

Solid Self-Worth:

CONFIDENCE IS THE OPPOSITE OF NARCISSISM

Here's an understatement: Being a teenager is not easy. The group politics, hormonal shifts, physical changes, family dynamics, all the new pressures and temptations. Like most adolescents, I had some wonky times. It was no picnic, and this was before the exacerbating, nonstop parade of comparison and vulnerable exposure of social media.

When I was asked by a chapter of the Boys and Girls Club to lead journaling workshops for high schoolers, I spent some time mind-traveling back to my own teen years. I journaled, dreaming onto the page what I wish I could've told a teenage version of myself. What knowledge bombs and life hacks did I want to whisper into her ear to save her time and heartache? That list was initially long, but a simple, overarching theme emerged. I wanted to help these teens connect to their own worth, to the unique attributes that made them who they were, and to their ability to appreciate themselves.

Teenagers tend to police each other; jealousy is a daily hazard. Step away from the pack and you're potentially exposing yourself to cruelty and ridicule. "She's so obsessed with herself; it's actually sad." "He really has no reason to be that cocky." "It's cute you think you're so smart." And far worse. It's difficult to feel secure in your own particular flavor of greatness when you're waiting for someone to knock you down a peg or three.

This unfortunate dynamic isn't limited to teens; it's an underlying, insidious belief system that follows us into adulthood. Part of the problem is a misconception that feeling too good about yourself is a punishable offense. In Australia, the dynamic has a name: tall poppy syndrome.[1] The idea is that when one flower in the field grows too tall, above the others, it'll be cut down to size as a way of condemning outsize ego. And we're the flowers. Ouch. The message here is, "Don't shine too brightly, or we'll take you out." Not exactly a winning operating system for creativity and personal development.

But healthy confidence shouldn't be confused with arrogance. It's not as if "too much" self-esteem turns you into an insufferable jerk. In fact, self-worth is actually the opposite of self-absorbed vanity. Displays of puffed-up ego compensate for deep feelings of inadequacy.[2] On the other end of the spectrum is self-respect. When you already know you're pretty great, it's actually a lot easier to be relaxed and modest because you aren't thirsting for acclaim. Instead of competing and comparing, you gravitate toward more enriching territory—meaningful connections, open dialogue, and real intimacy.

We're not here to play small in order to avoid upsetting poppy-cutting haters. That robs the world of our finest contributions, and it needs that stuff. Advancement is fueled by those who are brave enough to push past assumptions and challenge existing programming. There is no innovation without risk.

Here's a prompt that can help you nurture inner bravery. I hope it will embolden you to be more fully and exceptionally yourself. Sometimes a shift in behavior can begin with a vision, and knowing the general coordinates of where you want to head can help a whole lot.

PROMPT: The idea of "daring to dare" is essential in creating an expansive, rewarding life. Let's journal into that space. *What would you do if you were more daring?* Here are some categories for you to explore as you consider the prompt. Pick whichever ones speak to you, or add your own.

- Professionally
- Romantically
- Financially
- Creatively
- Spiritually
- As a parent
- As a friend
- As a partner
- As an individual
- As a citizen

Envision what you want to call in—for yourself, your loved ones, your community, even the world at large. Go granular, go big, and everything in between. Write for ten to twelve minutes, but keep going if there's more to say. Try not to veer into negative self-talk or overthink the exercise. Write from your gut and be bold.

My version of personal excellence may not look much like yours. I'm no triathlete, and you definitely don't want me doing anyone's taxes, but I've come to appreciate (and even celebrate) my own mix of traits and strengths. It took me a lot of miles to arrive at this vista. I can't go back in time to have a heart-to-heart with the teen me, to convey my earned perspective. But I could share it with the teenagers of the Boys and Girls Club, and I can share it with you. Let's see whatcha got. Go big, my friend. I dare you.

31

Corporal Incorporated:

BODY: CONSCIOUS

Self-care stress is real. Ironic, I know. Nonetheless, it's difficult to navigate which new vitamin protocol, fasting style, detox tool, injectable peptide, or wearable technology will make a substantial difference to your health and wellness. Often these commodities and techniques are marketed as The Solution, the fix we've always needed but didn't know about until it was packaged and sold to us. (Is organic sea moss gel really what we've been missing all this time?) Wellness overwhelm may occur when your self-care to-do list becomes so lengthy that you could spend your whole morning ticking through it. Separating hype from reality, I've been able to identify what actually works for me by tracking how I feel in the pages of a notebook.

Your journal can become a valuable tool to help you get the most out of professional medical input. Case in point: My first home in California was a sweet little beach bungalow. It was agave green with white trim, had a shaded front porch where I sat and journaled in the morning. It was the place in the world where I felt most calm and centered. But I had no idea that it was making me sick.

I take good care of my body. It's been through a lot, and I'm keen to keep everything working well. Within two years of moving in, I'd started to feel terrible despite my best efforts. The symptoms didn't show up overnight, but my health began to decline. I became exhausted, hampered by brain fog, constantly sick with viral infections, and eventually my face and body grew pallid and puffy. My belly was distended, my digestion was wildly off, and I was so tired I could only do one activity per day. At the zenith of this mysterious malaise, the exertion of a trip to the grocery store meant I didn't have any remaining energy left to cook a meal.

I knew something was wrong but was unable to wrest a diagnosis out of any kind of medical provider. Frustrated and flummoxed, I turned to the tool that has repeatedly been my saving grace. Rather than only looking for answers from external sources, I connected with my own counsel via my journal. Nobody had recognized any correlation with my environment until I started to log symptoms on the page. Each day I wrote down the date, where I was in the world, and how I felt. Patterns emerged. I started to track back, identifying when my ailments had shown up and at which points they'd intensified.

My journal connected important dots and told the story. I'd been bicoastal for a few years but had been gradually transitioning to the West Coast as my home base. When I was on the road for work, I might be jet-lagged and maxed on output, but despite those physical stressors, I was far healthier than when I was parked in Los Angeles, unwinding. I finally realized the origin point of my deterioration was when I'd made Venice Beach my full-time address.

I'd heard stories about toxic mold from friends in my local community. The charming bungalows of the neighborhood were made for mild, dry, seventy-two-and-sunny days, not the wetter, colder bouts of weather that climate change has introduced. But it wasn't until the key piece of data clicked into place (thanks to journaling) that I had any inkling toxic mold was my undesirable roommate. I did some research, and one urinalysis later, the results were unequivocal. Yup, I had mold poisoning.

By all accounts, I was outrageously lucky. I've been able to reverse my mold toxicity by moving house, the intervention of a gastroenterologist, and the sage care of a functional medicine practitioner. I'm now symptom free and off medication, and my quality of life is excellent. I manage my gut health with a combination of diet and supplements. I miss gluten but not as much as I don't miss all those former ailments.

If I'd continued to live in an environment that was harming me, the outcome would have probably been very different. This is another example of why I have journaling to thank for my well-being.

PROMPT: We often need to be our own health advocates, and a notebook is a great ally. If something's up and you're not quite sure what it is, start a wellness tracker. You can incorporate elements such as:

- Food (what you ate and when): to see if there are dietary triggers.
- Symptoms (how you feel, what time and where): noting shifts for the better or the worse.

- Sleep (how long and well you sleep, any naps, how you feel upon waking).

- Water intake (how much you drink in a day): to monitor hydration, a frequent cause of exhaustion.

- Movement (how active you've been): exercise type and intensity, and how well you recovered.

- Boosters (such as acupuncture, vitamin drips, herbs, hormones, etc.): whatever you've undertaken to improve your well-being, both allopathic (conventional) and otherwise.

Start with what aspect(s) seem amiss, but it's just as important to note when you're feeling good and the circumstances correlated with that. Consistency is key. You can zero in on whether that acupuncturist is working out for you, if those B vitamins are what's making your stomach wonky, or if glutathione is indeed your personal hero.

Investigating our personal-health matrix—the elements that make us feel, look, sleep, and perform well—is a valuable inquiry. We now have loads of apps and wearable-technology options to help us gather data. If you find some of these resources to be illuminating, great. But remember that they are usually designed to parse out specific sets of information, looking through only one lens, which often leads to missed connections (such as location, in my case). Using technology alongside your notebook can help to integrate various sources of data. Add their findings to your analog, pen-to-paper wellness notebook. Cumulatively, you'll become an expert on your own health.

Moreover, answering the question "How am I feeling today?" shouldn't be deferred to an external source. I instituted an in-bed, body-scan journaling practice in the morning as a way of turning a literal page rather than turning to tech at this precious time of day.

PROMPT: I like to do this lying down in the morning or at night in bed, but you don't have to. Sitting comfortably works, too. Relax and take a few deep, slow, and centering breaths. From feet to scalp (or from tip to toe, if you prefer heading south), witness how your body feels, part by part and globally. Notice whatever sensations are present: heat, cold, discomfort, ease, stiffness, relaxed suppleness. Jot it down in your journal. Or if you prefer, draw an outline of a figure and use it as a template to show what you're feeling. Then ask yourself what your body needs. What would help support its optimal state of health?

To be crystal clear, I'm not suggesting that you skip out on consulting medical professionals. I've been an extremely fortunate beneficiary of the best of what modern medicine provides, and I've also tried out alternative modalities to optimize my health. I recommend availing yourself of both if you can. But nobody else can tell you how you feel.

You are in your body. By tracking its nuances, you're empowered with information you can share with your health care providers, rather than ceding your corporal knowledge to external systems. After all, it's your body—not theirs. Journaling helps us become empowered advocates for our own health.

32

The Breakup Handbook:

HOW TO HEAL IN THE WAKE OF HEARTBREAK

My client was in tears. Not delicate, translucent pearls rolling down the cheeks kind of tears. She was in full sob mode. She had a creative coaching session scheduled with me, but reached out beforehand, candidly sharing that she was in the midst of a breakup breakdown. She asked if we should reschedule, but I gently suggested that this would probably be the perfect time for a mindful journaling session.

We spent the hour doing some supportive pen-to-paper activities and talking through the physiological reasons why breakups are so hard. For that, blame the chemicals. Romantic love provides us with an IV drip of delicious hormones and neurotransmitters, including noradrenaline[1] (which stimulates adrenaline production, often providing a "rush"); dopamine (pure pleasure),[2] phenylethylamine[3] (released when we're near our crush, giving us "butterflies"), and oxytocin[4] (the cuddle hormone that provides a sense of tranquility). That's some seriously potent stuff, the loss of which can tumble us into a form of withdrawal.[5] Understanding this dynamic doesn't necessarily diminish the heartache, but it can helpfully reframe it.

Long-form anguish writing is the little black dress of journaling, a classic approach. Just write and write and write your heart out. You may or may not feel immediately "lighter" for having done it, but this is immensely healthy for your long-term well-being. You can process here, say the unsayable. And, hey, maybe you will want to rip those pages out and straight up burn them? Be safe in that process, but it's pretty satisfying to watch all that melt away into the ether.

Another reason to embrace analog journaling during such a highly emotional time is that one-way communication can be an ally. Step away from your keyboard and channel your emotions into your notebook instead. This is infinitely better than texting the object of your affection multiple paragraphs in the middle of the night. And this is vastly more dignified than offering up half-digested thoughts and feelings to someone who may or may not appreciate them. You're sparing yourself any vulnerability hangovers.

There are plenty of other ways to leverage your journal during such a charged time, and none of them involve revenge dating or large quantities of ice cream. Here are some of my mindful journaling prescriptions to help heal heartbreak.

- **Get organized. Maybe there are things to say that will help provide meaningful closure. Instead of an unedited, fire hose approach,** write your thoughts down. Get clear on the page. Then share that perspective with your former partner (or don't—your call!) in whatever way/s are most appropriate—in writing, in person, over the phone, etc. But by writing it all down *first*, you're more likely to have a productive and healing dialogue. Give yourself the chance to regain some clarity around your own narrative, whether or not you're sharing it.

- **You rock.** A relationship rupture can feel like rejection, but not all unions are built to last. Apparently, this person isn't your person for the long haul. Okay, so be it. Doesn't mean you're not lovable (spoiler alert: you are lovable).

  When was the last time you claimed your amazingness? Write down things every day that you appreciate about yourself. They can be big and small. Triple down on self-worth. Start noticing when you veer into negative self-talk, and when that happens, go back to the list of your awesomeness. This isn't "I'm fluent in six languages and have abs you can bounce a quarter off of" territory. If that's you, God bless. It sure isn't me. Maybe you make a damn fine cup of coffee, you parallel park like a boss, or you're a really good listener, whatever! And keep adding to that list on an ongoing basis.

- **Run yourself a (chemical) bath.** Whether or not the union was as great as the promise it held, in a breakup, we're letting go of both companionship and its fantasy. That's hard enough, but with all the aforementioned substances streaming out of your system, it's even harder. You don't have to go cold turkey. (No, I'm not talking about breakup sex.) There are boatloads of other healthy activities that can help you replace a rush of pleasure. One of the best ways to build stairs out of this hole is to dream up other things that provide good vibes, then do them. While wallowing has both its place and appeal, you will feel less rotten if you step away from Netflix,

I promise. So, sketch out a plan, write down things that provide a shot (or even a blip) of buoyancy, and get after them. (BTW: This works any time, not just when you're going through a heart mend, which is why it's got its own chapter, Dopamine Push-Ups, in Part 2 of this book.)

All good and proven advice but here's the numero uno, top pro tip I can provide. It may sound counterintuitive because it isn't about you directly, but it works.

PROMPT: Help someone. Write ways in which you can be of service, and go be useful. This is the best way I've found to feel better during really lousy times: to move beyond my own self-oriented pain. Spend time thinking about—and supporting—someone other than yourself, and be amazed at how much better the day becomes. We're wired to feel good when we help others.[6]

Need a running start? Some ideas to spark your own:

- What is a charity that's meaningful for you? (If you're not sure, do a bit of research.) Reach out and see what they need, where you might be able to help. It's ideal if it's hands-on, but it might be something less tangible, like fundraising. All of it counts. Make a donation, start a fundraiser on your social media, spread the word about their mission and needs.

- Find ways to be of service to your immediate community, be it a friend, a professional contact, or family member, whomever. It doesn't matter how big or small your act of generosity is. Not sure what to do? *Just ask.* "Hey, how are you? How can I help?" The inquiry itself might be medicine for the recipient. Note: It's often hard for someone to actually say what help they need, so follow-through is really important here.

- Think of someone who is in a bind, whose present circumstances are in some way/s lousier than yours. Identify ways you can make positive impacts by helping them out of a jam. And then do that—discreetly. Stock their fridge. Send them flowers. Pay their parking ticket. Not because of the acclaim, but because you can. Bask in the glow of your own quiet kindness.

While heartache can feel deeply personal, it's not just you. Pretty much everyone on this planet has felt or will feel some version of what you're feeling right now. From presidents to supermodels, CEOs, professional athletes, and members of Mensa, it's extremely rare that anyone travels through life entirely unscathed by romantic ruptures. It is part of being open to connection, and that is a gift worth embracing, despite its possible perils.

There is no switch to flip that will make the hurt vanish. When it comes to heartache, there's no way out but through. But with the help of your notebook, you can make it to the other side a little more swiftly, with a lot more grace, newfound self-worth, and an outlook that will have you poised to make good decisions in the future. After all, the longest-standing relationship you're going to have in your life is the one you're already in—with yourself.

33

Heavy Weather:

CULTIVATING PERSPECTIVE, EVEN IN A SQUALL

Sunny days make for good moods,[1] but storms are also inevitable. Sometimes it's just a bit of quick, cleansing rain, but destructive hurricanes do happen, literally and figuratively. When faced with large-scale life difficulties, the swirling kind that don't seem solvable, we are at a heightened risk of becoming disempowered, shutting down. To avoid overwhelm, I practice making space for the emotional equivalent of bluebird skies and storm clouds, not sequentially but *simultaneously*. It's possible to feel on-your-knees heartbreak and expansive gratitude at the same time. (I speak from personal experience here.) Even the hardest days have a bit of grace, especially when we're committed to seeking it out.

To help me be present to adversity and beauty within the same day—sometimes even within the same moment—I created this Daily Rose journaling activity. Because even the thorniest, spikiest days have some petals tucked in there somewhere. Use your pen and you can find them. The payoff is big—layers of appreciations, learning, and meaning.

PROMPT: Scan your day . . .

Thorn. Write down a problematic moment, something that frustrated you or brought you low. Here's your chance to wring it out. Venting longhand usually diminishes the thorn's sting and helps you develop the ability to regulate your emotions.[3] Then consider on the page, what meaning do you think the event has? Is a solution available? What can be done to address the hurdle, to lessen its impact? However, simply having written about it may be all the solution you need for now.

Bloom. Write down an instance of sweetness, a win, even a small joy from your day. What impact did it have? Where were you? How did it make you feel? If you're having trouble identifying something positive today, here are questions to consider:

- What was the warmest, most connected moment you had, and why?
- Even if you weren't the direct recipient, where did you witness beauty or kindness?
- At what point did you feel most alive?

You don't need to give both elements exactly equal airtime, but try to balance it out. And I suggest starting this duo with the thorn, so you finish up the exercise in a positive frame of mind.

Tracking your days in this way can reveal patterns and "story arcs" that play out repeatedly. What unexpected elements bring you joy? What keeps tripping you up? Recognizing these tendencies is powerful knowledge that you can employ to minimize friction and amplify joy. By regularly compiling these roses, you're gathering together a kind of flawed but gorgeous bouquet.

The irony is that, while this prompt creates duality, what comes into focus is a lot more nuanced. As humans, we have incredible emotional range.[4] Letting our internal life be a large enough container to hold all kinds of sentiments—triumph, envy, adoration, nostalgia, disgust, discovery, and so much more—is a gift you're giving yourself. By bringing attention to daily blooms and busts, we stretch our capacity to be present to both the difficulties we are going through and the enduring sweetness of life.

Complex problems require complex solutions. In order to help us imagine those remedies into being, we need to stay inspired, even when the odds aren't looking great. On some of my darkest days, this is the prompt I invoke to nourish my psyche and spirit.

PROMPT: How did love show up for you today (so far)? List all the big and small ways. Write for six minutes about love, however you care to define it. Please let's not limit ourselves to romance, which is just one of a whole bunch of ways love exists. There's so much more: Pet love. Friend love. Self-love. Tree love. Sibling love. Mentor love. Love from a stranger or a neighbor. How did love work its way into your day?

This exercise helps me reclaim my equilibrium. Recognizing love might not be the answer to every problem, but it's a very good place to start, whatever the weather.

34

Good Grief:

WRITING THROUGH LOSS

The call came in the afternoon. "Your father had an incident. We think it was a heart attack. Come to the hospital as fast as you can." I sped toward that address with everything I had. By the time I arrived, he was already gone.

I didn't understand. I had spoken to him the day before. He was there, material. But somehow, mind-bendingly, he was now *not* there. My fit, tennis-playing father—who we thought would outlive us all—had evaporated in an instant. His personality, energy, wit, and intelligence had entirely vanished by some perverse, irreversible magic trick.

The intense shock of his absence initially left me numb—then it roared. Grief flayed me open, entering my bones and blood; it occupied my mind and operated my soul. At times, I didn't know how I would breathe. (Was I breathing? How odd.) I sleepwalked with eyes open through the sea of paperwork, decisions, and rituals that follow a death. I was on this earth, but not entirely. Part of me was always with my dad, ricocheting toward him in the beyond.

In the years that followed, the love for my father that emanated from the deepest wells within me was so fine and true that it had an almost crystalline quality. My grief was more real than the tea in my cup, the dollars in my bank account, the toothbrush I dutifully used twice daily. What was any of that worth now that my father had gone?

That grief is still the purest love I have ever known. It wasn't needy; there was no hope of it ever being reciprocated. It spilled out of my chest in generous waves with nowhere to go, reaching for a shore that would never materialize. I prayed into the cosmos that the messages of my heart would somehow be received. I prayed into the dark that my father's spirit could perceive the scale of my appreciation and respect. "Hear me. Please. Dear, God, please let him hear me." *I love you, I love you, I love you*, I'd repeat over and over in my head and heart, like a homing signal. I think I was half mad at times.

The fog took years to lift. And when it started to dissipate, I clung to it because this pain was the only remaining proof of my proximity to my father.

That was over a decade ago. The fever dream has released its grip. In its place is a connection that time cannot fade, one I cherish and savor. Grief and I have become friends; there's a civility to most of our interactions now, replacing its former unchecked ferocity. A truce has been called, though I'm still not entirely sure by whom. Maybe by me, or perhaps my father's spirit put in a good word somewhere.

While I'm your journaling guide, in the territory of grief I'm also very much a peer. I've stumbled along this path, so your footsteps behind mine are familiar. I wrote my way through my experience, clinging to my pen like a buoy. I dearly hope some of the solace I found on the page will also be soothing and healing for you.

One source of my heartache was a fear that memories of my father would fade away. A gratifying way of keeping the memory of our loved ones alive is by telling stories about them—especially the poignant, funny, and beautiful ones. When a friend has recently experienced loss, I ask them to share a favorite reminiscence with me, to say out loud the name of the person who passed. It provides an opportunity to celebrate their loved one through storytelling. This writing exercise operates in a similar way.

PROMPT: Pick a heartening memory you associate with your late loved one, something that brings you joy, that makes you smile (even if you're smiling through tears). Take a moment to pick a positive reminiscence, then journal about it. "That time when . . ."

Explore this on the page for as much time as it takes, but please don't get hung up on doing the recollection literary justice. Instead, give yourself permission to wander through the memory, calling up bits of imagery. Try using your senses as a device to access details. What were you seeing, hearing, tasting, smelling, feeling during this scene?

For example, I associate the sound of baseball on the radio with my father, as well as the smell of a fresh can of tennis balls, the act of pulling the lever at the voting booth, the rustle of expertly folding the Sunday paper. In all these things, he is with me. Through writing, I was able to identify these moments as emblems of his continued presence in my life.

I return to this exercise when I'm hit by a wave of missing my dad. It provides an action to take, something to *do* rather than getting submerged in my grief. I encourage you to try it out. In doing so, you're deepening your relationship with these treasured memories and creating a tribute to your loved one in the process.

Part of what's so confounding about loss is the lack of communication with the person who has moved on. You have all these emotions—towering amounts of love, things that didn't get said (but maybe should have), even old resentments that need airing, etc.—with nowhere to put them.

It's common to write a letter to someone who has passed as a way of getting closure. Letters provide a potent container, regardless of whether they're sent. If you haven't tried it, I recommend it as a cathartic practice. I write to my dad when I have something to tell him or questions for him. In the writing, I often find my answer. But here, we are going to turn that premise inside out.

PROMPT: Try out writing a letter *from* your loved one *to* you. Use your imagination to tune into their voice. What do you think they'd like to communicate? What additional wisdom or pieces of information do you think they want to share now that they're in the great beyond? Maybe they want to tell you they're okay, or they're proud of you. Or that they miss you, too, but they're not nearly so far away as you might think. Maybe they want to apologize. Let their voice show up on the page and say whatever it is they want to say.

I recommend giving yourself the grace of at least ten minutes to explore this prompt, but take whatever time you need. And if this exercise is too emotionally raw for you right now, please don't force it. If it's too intense or you're feeling blocked, you can try swapping it around and write to them first. Start there and shift over to their response whenever you're ready. Maybe tomorrow, maybe next month, or some other time in the future.

When you're done writing your letter, check in with yourself to help integrate the experience. Was it difficult, powerful, beautiful, bittersweet? Did what showed up surprise you at all? What did you learn?

Writing from or to your loved one can become an ongoing ritual. It's possible to develop it into a kind of epistolary conversation, or you can just tap the device of a letter whenever you're craving their departed voice—wishing you could share some great news, asking for advice, recounting an occurrence that brought them to mind, etc. In their absence, bring it to the page.

Elisabeth Kübler-Ross identified five stages of grief: denial, anger, bargaining, depression, and acceptance.[1] David Kessler, an expert on grief and Kübler-Ross's coauthor of *On Grief and Grieving*,[2] went on to document a sixth stage: finding meaning. He suggests that, while many people look for closure after a loss, meaning transforms grief into a more peaceful and hopeful experience.[3]

I came across a stunning example of this quite by accident. In December 2019, I went to Walden Woods for a little field trip. Henry David Thoreau famously wrote the naturalist masterpiece *Walden* in a tiny ten-foot by nineteen-foot cottage he constructed as a shelter on this property. I first read the book in high school, but it wasn't until I toured the grounds that I learned one of the surprising, personal reasons Thoreau took to the woods.

He had been so overwhelmed with loss after the death of his brother, John, that he had to withdraw from the life he knew. For over two years, Thoreau maintained a life of simplicity and reflection apart from society. His journals from that time resulted in *Walden*. But the trail of meaning doesn't end there.

Thoreau's profound grief, which he poured into his journals, transmuted into a global web of advocacy. In 1862, explorer John Muir read *Walden*, which spurred Muir's advocacy for wilderness protection and contributed to the formation of America's National Park System. One hundred years later, author Rachel Carson was influenced by Thoreau's words and published *Silent Spring*, which galvanized an environmental movement against the use of harmful pesticides and chemicals.[4] *Walden* established Thoreau as an author, and encouraged by its publication, he published an essay, "On the Duty of Civil Disobedience," which would be read by both Gandhi[5] and Martin Luther King Jr.[6] Each credited the essay as an immense source of inspiration for his own nonviolent approaches to resisting oppression. In effect, all of this miraculous change—from the National Park System to the civil rights movement in America—is in part attributed to the memory of Thoreau's late brother, John. That's a whole lot of meaning wrung from loss.

"Out of despair, one creates. What else can one do?" wisely counseled Elie Wiesel. With creativity and meaning as our allies, here is an exercise for you to check out when you are ready.

PROMPT: Maybe not today, but whenever you're motivated to explore this theme, open your notebook and consider the way/s in which you might channel your grief into creative acts. A poem, an op-ed, a short film (or a film screening)? Maybe it's a champagne picnic at one of the spots a departed person enjoyed, or a food drive for a local pantry? Whatever mediums and outlets speak to you, go organize, activate, and create on behalf of your late loved one. Maybe it will benefit your family, friends, or your community—or even people well beyond your community. But it doesn't have to. The act of creating anything inspired by the love for and loss of your loved ones is ample enough reason.

The club of loss is real. If, like me, you're a member, I hope you'll find your way to the page. Stuck grief can get "lodged" in the body. Writing helps release some of the physical manifestation of our grieving, easing its intensity.[7] Mindful journaling doesn't bring back the person we've lost, but it keeps them close. I no longer have access to my father, but through writing, he's still one of my trusted advisers. An element of intimacy remains, and I know he would be pleased that his memory helped fuel this chapter. In essence, you're my creative collaborator. In reading, you've helped me unlock meaning.

35

In Praise of the Long Game:

STEADFAST AND FRUITFUL

When a poet moves to a place called Haiku, it's bound to result in a good story. In my wanderings, I've been fortunate to spend time at the Merwin Conservancy's palm sanctuary in Haiku, Maui. Visiting there taught me what one (dedicated) person can accomplish.

In 1976, poet William S. Merwin took a piece of Hawaiian land that had been destroyed and left for dead by shortsighted corporate agriculture and brought it back to thriving life. But that didn't happen overnight.

First, Merwin planted 1,000 diverse native plants with his own hands. They all died. Every. Single. One.

A thousand different failures. Despite that outcome, he didn't quit. Instead, he turned his efforts specifically to palms, which are technically part of the grass family. They are "vascular tubes" rather than trees, scientifically speaking.

He planted and planted. Many of the palms died, but some lived.

Forty years later, over 2,740 hand-planted palms representing more than 400 species (including some exceedingly rare and sought after "holy grail palms") are thriving in this former wasteland. It's now lush and abundant, pulsing with green life and all that comes with it; I had the mosquito bites to prove it.

The nineteen-acre forest is a living, three-dimensional poem—a testament to vision, patience, and grit. And W. S. Merwin is no slouch when it comes to words, either. He's a two-time Pulitzer Prize–winning U.S. poet laureate.[1]

Welcome to the long game: seemingly small changes that yield exponential results over time, with repetition, perseverance, and consistency. Long-game vision is about delayed yields, but it's served by having faith in the process despite not being able to peek around the corner. Sometimes the most pivotal experiences in our lives come in the form of "pink slips" or other unwelcome containers. Or they are events that we hardly notice at all. Only looking back can we see that the innocuous occurrence was actually a redirect.

Here's an exercise to help you better appreciate some of your own story, witnessing where the long game has been supporting you all along.

PROMPT: What are some of the experiences, interactions, and learnings in your life that eventually paid off in ways you couldn't have seen or expected? At the time, maybe you thought they were incidental, a waste, or even a failure. But in retrospect, you can see how pivotal they've been. Pick one and spend some time with it. Write for ten minutes about what it was and the delayed value it created.

Whether or not you believe in fate, looking back can help you have more trust in your present. Because here you are. You made it this far, thanks in part to those bad days and benign occurrences when you listened to your gut or honored your creative impulses.

Without short-term indications of success, being dedicated over an extended time frame, particularly amidst our age of distraction and correlating attention spans, isn't easy. But it has a big payoff. When asked why he planted a palm forest, W. S. Merwin responded, "I can't stop them from destroying the Amazon forest, but I can go out and plant a tree, you know?"[2] He did what he could where he could and was steadfast in his goal.

Positive change is possible, despite how barren and defeated the terrain may appear. Take Merwin's palm forest as proof. That's true externally and internally: silencing the critical voice, building self-respect, reframing anxiety, becoming a more joyful, self-actualized, and creatively expressed version of yourself. Even a few minutes a day of putting pen to paper will help, but staying committed to the practice is where the biggest unlock is waiting. Planting one palm is good; planting 3,000 palms is better—just like journaling once in a while is helpful, but consistency has exponential rewards.

Stay the course. It works, even if at times wandering around on the page feels fruitless and you don't see any proof of progress. The process *is* progress. In time, you'll be able to look back and see how you used this simple yet revolutionary tool to transform your life into a lush, verdant ecosystem.

36

Headliners Need Help:

RUGGED INDIVIDUALISM IS OVERRATED

I've got it" is one of my default defense mechanisms. When I'm afraid of someone dropping a ball and disappointing me or leaving me in a lurch, I cowgirl up and get the task done myself. And sure, sometimes this self-reliance has served me well, but not always. There are plenty of instances when being gracious about letting people show up, where and how they can, would have made the road a lot less arduous.

Accepting assistance isn't some kind of personal shortcoming. It enables you to operate at your best. So, if you're aiming for stoicism, please think again. Going it alone might be limiting your vision, playing small when instead you could be playing arenas.

Even rock stars need roadies. And the bigger the venue, the more help they need. Headliners can't be on stage performing if they're also driving the bus, rigging the stage, running the soundboards, selling the merch, taking the tickets, cueing the lights, making sure all the gear is loaded in and out, etc. They need a slew of experts to plan a tour and move them from venue to venue. All the people on that team have their own areas of excellence, and when everything is humming along, the team enables the artist to really deliver the goods—to provide a transformative and inspiring creative experience at scale.

Whether you're navigating tough times or launching yourself into a new adventure (or some combination thereof), community can see you through. This writing prompt helps you build out your team.

PROMPT: What kinds of assistance do you need or want? Who or what can support your personal goals? Maybe it's behind-the-scenes support so you're freed up to take center stage? Or, conversely, perhaps you need a front man to round out your team and boost sales? It can be mundane or elevated—a dog walker, babysitter, mentor, therapist, graphic designer, a new laptop, travel agent, copywriter, bookkeeper, endocrinologist, angel investor, trademark lawyer, virtual assistant, a pack of personal training sessions, etc.

Bear in mind, you don't have to know exactly the right person or resource just yet. If you do, that's great. If not, start by naming the kinds of help you'd most benefit from ("A virtual part-time assistant would be life changing"), and you can identify specifics later. For example, you might want to grow your start-up business and have identified that a capital infusion might be the best way forward, but you aren't currently connected to any angel investors or venture capital firms. Once you know you're ready to explore taking on investment, you can start inquiring through your networks and researching. Take at least ten minutes to consider where you could use help, and write it down.

One way to do this is to scan a typical day or week. At what points do you tend to run into snags? Where do things get muddled, and what could change that scenario? Also worth considering is where your existing resources are ready for an upgrade. If your fancy coffee machine keeps breaking, it might be time to swap it for a simple French press. That might be enough to put the "good" back in your good morning.

Congratulations, you have started to assemble your cadre of experts and resources! If that's all you needed from this chapter, you can stop here. In case you're unclear about next steps or feel a little overwhelmed by the scope of your own needs, I have some additional, optional steps. Too much simultaneous change (even the beneficial sort) can create its own kind of stress, so here are a couple of different ways to help you implement things incrementally.

PROMPT:

APPROACH 1. Go through your list and pick out low-hanging fruit. Which of these will be relatively easy to activate? Pick three and circle them. You're going to implement those first. Choose a time frame for yourself (two days, two weeks, two months?) and put it in your calendar. Once you've got the first three done, pick three more, and repeat the process.

APPROACH 2. After rereading your journal entry, choose which three elements will make the biggest positive impact. Just three. Move each to the top of a new page. And spend three minutes exploring each one. Who do you know who might be able to make introductions or provide a referral? Drill down into what the "ask" looks like—why you are looking for this kind of support.

Even if you're not clear on exactly what the next steps are, you have now identified what you need, and you'll be more likely to spot it when it comes your way.

Philosophically, I applaud intellectual and creative independence, but I know that, in reality, the execution of ideas often takes many hands. Our culture celebrates rugged individualism, romanticizing cowboys sleeping under the stars. But in reality, those cowboys move cattle by working in teams, not all by their lonesome.

And thank goodness we don't have to "lone wolf" it all the time, because life can be bone-achingly difficult. Hardships are made less so in community. Life can also be exquisitely, gloriously sublime. Thankfully, we don't experience those instances exclusively alone, either. Because our best moments are so much sweeter when shared.

37

Deceptively Divine:

"COMING OUT" AS A CONSCIOUS CREATIVE

Late one night, I was having a conversation with one of my mentors and shared something that had been quietly troubling me, like a stubborn pebble in my shoe. When I designed the AllSwell approach to journaling, I'd carefully chosen to avoid any mention whatsoever of a universal life force, a great knowing, steering clear of any spiritual trappings. Despite my personal, pantheistic belief that creativity and divinity are closely linked, I'd staunchly left God out of the brochure.

I wondered aloud if I was denying my true nature and, worse, withholding a valuable concept from my professional community. While access to the divine was right there in the act of journaling, I certainly wasn't calling anyone's attention to it. I hid the medicine in the mashed potatoes.

There's a quote often attributed to iconic country music singer-songwriter Hank Williams Sr., which pretty much sums up my perspective on the interplay between spirit and creativity: "I don't write the songs. I just hold the pen." Whether you call it communing, channeling, interpreting, or something else, it all emanates from the same unseen source. From Michelangelo to Bruce Springsteen, creatives through time have cited receiving ideas, images, lyrics, concepts, stanzas, and more from the big beyond—sometimes even fully formed. Then they have to go make the thing.

That's a handy consideration. Yet I'd stashed spirituality well out of sight. I instinctively felt it could trip up newbies—distract or repel them. As a result, I've been fortunate to bring journaling to some highly unlikely settings and demographics, including Wall Street bankers, corporate executives, technologists, special forces veterans, and venture capitalists—people who probably would've never otherwise journaled as catharsis, accessing it as a way to be reflective and derive more meaning from their lives.

This "build a big enough tent for everyone" approach is central to my fundamental objective. To effect a mindful writing revolution, we're going to need more than just the likely suspects to participate. I don't only want to engage with people who already have spiritual awareness and tools to support it (though my fellow travelers are most welcome at the writing table). My intent is to reach as many people as possible, especially those who need it most. Let's get *the jerks* journaling, too. They'll probably be a lot less jerky as a direct result—a win for everyone.

Back to my late-night discussion with one of my elders. I brought this quandary to him and half expected he'd say I was out of alignment, that publicly extolling the spiritual aspects of journaling would be the next step. But this learned, experienced man didn't dole out judgments or advice. Instead, he asked questions to help guide me toward my own answer.

And it appeared. "I don't need to do God's PR" were the words that came out of my mouth. The exquisite truth is that, whether or not I shout from the rooftops that igniting creativity is a form of convening and collaborating with the divine, it happens anyhow. After all, a journal is really just another kind of altar.

PROMPT: Where and when have you experienced a spontaneous creative spark? An idea that seemed to drop out of the sky, words that found their way to you, an image that floated into your imagination. If you acted on it, where did that creative impulse take you? How did it play out?

Or if you ignored it in the moment, putting it aside "for later" or discounting its significance, how could you—now, today—honor it with your attention?

And next time the spark comes to play, how will you RSVP to that divine invitation?

ACKNOWLEDGMENTS

I wrote this book by myself, but I didn't do it alone. Logistical, emotional, and moral support has been provided by a platoon of people, pets, and carbohydrates.

Let's take it from the top. My mother intuited my need for a creative outlet and gave me my first journal when I was seven. She showed me, by example, that paper held answers. I watched her problem-solve by sitting down at the dining room table with an oversize sketch pad, organizing her thoughts on the page. As a kiddo, I was regularly her plus-one at cultural events. The artists and curators were her friends, part of her life, and so, by extension, part of mine. Collectively these experiences instilled a respect for the creative act as something alive and accessible, not just behind glass at a museum.

A man of arts and letters, my father once told me, "We are people of the book." And he lived that. Sportswriter, journalist, editor, and publisher, he dedicated his career to the written word. I miss him every day, but he was very close to me during the entire process of conceiving and writing this book.

My brother, the North Star who taught me that I steer my own ship.

From early days, when I had an outlier idea in seed form, I have been very fortunate to have some first-rate thinkers and doers as co-conspirators, including: Alessandra Olanow, Dr. Monisha Vasa, Adam and Kate Rosante, Celia Chen, Kassia Meador, Jessica Hundley, Jen Sison, Jun Lee, Allison Kunath, Katerina Siminova, Sara Reistad-Long, Joyce Englander, Michelle Swavely, Sarah Rigano, Randi Packard, Emily Nathan, Tom Werney, Brynn Kenny, Lex Weinstein, Kim Ficaro, Allison Ochmanek, Eddie Berrang, Katherine Danesi, Heidi Zumbrun, Alexandra Cassaniti, Liz Clark, Leah Dawson, Zach Weisberg, Shaney Jo Darden, Mark Tesi, Julie Goldstein, Beth O'Rourke, Ted Harrington, Sadie Adams, and so many more talented humans. I humbly thank you all for your wisdom, talent, time, and support.

Most especially, thanks to Joy Tutela and Veronica Alvarado for believing.

And my personal life raft: Jennifer Grass, Tanisha Christie, Megan Johnson, and the 4-pack: Juliet Clapp, Stacy Mackler, and Stephanie Sanborn. But I really cannot imagine how I would have gotten through all those hours in the library without Giles and Charlie to come home to.

NOTES

INTRODUCTION

1. Deloitte, "2025 digital media trends: Social platforms are becoming a dominant force in media and entertainment," *Deloitte Insights* (March 25, 2025), https://www2.deloitte.com/us/en/insights/industry/technology/digital-media-trends-consumption-habits-survey/2025.html.

2. "Survey: 1 in 4 adults checks phone less than a minute after waking up," *StudyFinds* (October 17, 2018), https://studyfinds.org/survey-quarter-checks-phones-less-than-minute-after-waking/.

CHAPTER ONE: THE GURU IS YOU

1. M. Korte, "The impact of the digital revolution on human brain and behavior: Where do we stand?" *Dialogues in Clinical Neuroscience* 22, no. 2 (2020): 101–111, doi:10.31887/DCNS.2020.22.2/mkorte.

CHAPTER THREE: FREE-RANGE JOURNALING

1. M. Sohal, "Efficacy of journaling in the management of mental illness: A systematic review and meta-analysis," *Family Medicine and Community Health* 10, no. 1 (2022): e001154, doi:10.1136/fmch-2021-001154.

CHAPTER FOUR: AN ON-RAMP

1. B. Kowalski, *bonitappétit*, accessed June 6, 2025, https://bonitappetit.substack.com.

2. M. Treadway and D. Zald, "Dopamine impacts your willingness to work," *Vanderbilt University News* (May 1, 2012), https://news.vanderbilt.edu/2012/05/01/dopamine-impacts-your-willingness-to-work/.

3. Name changed to protect identity.

4. Eric Sinclair, personal correspondence with author, May 25, 2024.

5. J. Keating, "Why time is a social construct," *Smithsonian Magazine* (January 2013),

https://www.smithsonianmag.com/science-nature/why-time-is-a-social-construct-164139110/.

CHAPTER FIVE: BY ANY MEANS NECESSARY

1. F. R. van der Weel and A. L. H. Van der Meer, "Handwriting but not typewriting leads to widespread brain connectivity: A high-density EEG study with implications for the classroom," *Frontiers in Psychology* 14 (2024): 1219945, doi:10.3389/fpsyg.2023.1219945.

2. P. A. Mueller and D. M. Oppenheimer, "The pen is mightier than the keyboard: Advantages of longhand over laptop note taking," *Psychological Science* 25, no. 6 (2014): 1159–1168, https://doi.org/10.1177/0956797614524581.

3. C. Lopez Lloreda, "Handwriting may boost brain connections more than typing does," *Science News* (January 26, 2024) , https://www.sciencenews.org/article/handwriting-brain-connections-learning.

4. A. Mangen et al., "Handwriting versus keyboard writing: Effect on word recall," *Journal of Writing Research* 7, no. 2 (2015): 227–247, https://doi.org/10.17239/jowr-2015.07.02.1.

CHAPTER TEN: MUCH MORE THAN COMPLAINING

1. This maxim was attributed to Disraeli by John Morley in the first of his three-volume *Life of William Ewart Gladstone* (1903): 222–223, according to the *Dictionary of Modern Proverbs* (2013).

2. A. N. Niles et al., "Randomized controlled trial of expressive writing for psychological and physical health: The moderating role of emotional expressivity, " *Anxiety, Stress, and Coping* 27, no. 1 (2014): 1–17, doi:10.1080/10615806.2013.802308.

3. R. Gupta and T. Vozar, "A psychological perspective on collective action and healing," *Psychotherapy Bulletin* 55, no. 1 (2020): 23–28.

CHAPTER ELEVEN: JOURNALING FOR BROS

1. E. Carbone et al., "He said, she said: Gender differences in the disclosure of positive and negative information," *Journal of Experimental Social Psychology* 110 (2024): 104525, https://doi.org/10.1016/j.jesp.2023.104525.

2. "Men less likely than women to share negative information, says study," Bayes Business School, University of London (November 6, 2023), https://www.bayes.citystgeorges.ac.uk/news-and-events/news/2023/november/men-less-likely-than-women-to-share-negative-information-says-study.

3. "Matthew Lieberman," UCLA Department of Psychology, accessed June 6, 2025, https://www.psych.ucla.edu/faculty-page/lieber/.

4. I. Sample, "Keeping a diary makes you happier," *Guardian* (February 15, 2009), https://www.theguardian.com/science/2009/feb/15/psychology-usa.

5. If you need professional help, please don't let stigma hold you back. A place to start

is Visible Man, which offers support groups and a podcast that address men's mental health issues; www.visibleman.org.

6. Another good place to start is NAMI, the National Alliance on Mental Illness, which offers peer-led support groups for any adult who has experienced symptoms of a mental-health condition; www.nami.org.

7. B. Gerrard et al., "Gay and straight men prefer masculine-presenting gay men for a high-status role: Evidence from an ecologically valid experiment," *Sex Roles* 88 (2023): 119–129, https://doi.org/10.1007/s11199-022-01332-y.

8. D. Ciampa, "The more senior your job title, the more you need to keep a journal," *Harvard Business Review* (July 7, 2017), https://danciampa.com/images/The%20More%20Senior%20Your%20Job%20Title%20the%20More%20You%20Need%20to%20Keep%20a%20Journal.pdf.

CHAPTER TWELVE: THE ATTENTION ECONOMY

1. "Multitasking: Switching costs," American Psychological Association, accessed June 6, 2025, https://www.apa.org/topics/research/multitasking.

2. F. Sana et al., "Laptop multitasking hinders classroom learning for both users and nearby peers," *Computers in Human Behavior* 52 (2015): 616–624, https://doi.org/10.1016/j.chb.2015.01.027.

3. J. S. Rubinstein et al., "Executive control of cognitive processes in task switching," *Journal of Experimental Psychology: Human Perception and Performance* 27, no. 4 (2001): 763–797, https://doi.org/10.1037/0096-1523.27.4.763.

4. R. Langner and S. B. Eickhoff, "Sustaining attention to simple tasks: A meta-analytic review of the neural mechanisms of vigilant attention," *Psychological Bulletin* 139, no. 4 (2013): 870–900, doi:10.1037/a0030694.

5. Y. Zhang et al., "The relationship between loneliness and mobile phone addiction among Chinese college students: The mediating role of anthropomorphism and moderating role of family support," *PLOS One* 18, no. 4 (April 28, 2023): e0285189, doi:10.1371/journal.pone.0285189.

6. S. Bhattacharya et al., "NOMOPHOBIA: NO MObile PHone PhoBIA," *Journal of Family Medicine and Primary Care* 8, no. 4 (2019): 1297–1300, doi:10.4103/jfmpc.jfmpc_71_19.

7. A. F. Ward et al., "Brain drain: The mere presence of one's own smartphone reduces available cognitive capacity," *Journal of the Association for Consumer Research* 2, no. 2 (2017): 140–154, https://doi.org/10.1086/691462.

8. M. Oliver, *Upstream: Selected Essays* (Penguin, 2016), p. 8.

CHAPTER THIRTEEN: HAPPY HOUR

1. E. Diener et al., "Beyond the hedonic treadmill: Revising the adaptation theory of well-being," *The American Psychologist* 61, no. 4 (2006): 305–314, doi:10.1037/0003-066X.61.4.305.

2. University of Rochester Medical Center, "Journaling for emotional wellness," *Health*

Encyclopedia, accessed July 8, 2025, https://www.urmc.rochester.edu/encyclopedia/content?ContentTypeID=1&ContentID=4552.

3. B. Chu et al., "Physiology, stress reaction" (updated May 7, 2024), National Library of Medicine, https://www.ncbi.nlm.nih.gov/books/NBK541120/.

4. "Oxytocin: The love hormone," Harvard Health Publishing, accessed July 7, 2025, https://www.health.harvard.edu/mind-and-mood/oxytocin-the-love-hormone.

5. E. S. Bromberg-Martin et al., "Dopamine in motivational control: Rewarding, aversive, and alerting," *Neuron* 68, no. 5 (2010): 815–834, doi:10.1016/j.neuron.2010.11.022.

6. S. Achor, *The Happiness Advantage: The Seven Principles of Positive Psychology That Fuel Success and Performance at Work* (Crown Business, 2010).

CHAPTER FOURTEEN: ANY TREE WILL DO

1. M. Monroy and D. Keltner, "Awe as a pathway to mental and physical health," *Perspectives on Psychological Science* 18, no. 2 (2022), https://doi.org/10.1177/17456916221094856.

2. R. Powers, *The Overstory* (W. W. Norton, 2018).

3. M. Dhar, "When did Earth's first forests emerge?" *Live Science* (July 2, 2022), https://www.livescience.com/when-did-first-forests-emerge.

4. University of Michigan, "Life Cycle of a Computer," Sustainable Computing, accessed June 6, 2025, https://sustainablecomputing.umich.edu/knowledge/life-cycle.php.

5. L. Delagran, "How does nature impact our wellbeing?" University of Minnesota (n.d.), https://www.takingcharge.csh.umn.edu/how-does-nature-impact-our-wellbeing.

6. K. E. Schertz and M. G. Berman, "Understanding nature and its cognitive benefits," *Current Directions in Psychological Science* 28, no. 5 (2019): 496–502, https://journals.sagepub.com/doi/10.1177/0963721419854100.

7. C.-W. Yeh et al., "The influence of natural environments on creativity," *Frontiers in Psychiatry* (July 27, 2022), https://pmc.ncbi.nlm.nih.gov/articles/PMC9363772/.

CHAPTER FIFTEEN: GET WET

1. University of British Columbia, "Effect of colors: Blue boosts creativity, while red enhances attention to detail," *ScienceDaily* (February 6, 2009), https://www.sciencedaily.com/releases/2009/02/090205142143.htm.

2. D. E. Dreher, "Surprising research on the color blue," *Psychology Today* (October 29, 2018), https://www.psychologytoday.com/us/blog/your-personal-renaissance/201810/surprising-research-on-the-color-blue.

3. R. Mehta and R. Zhu, "Blue or red? Exploring the effect of color on cognitive task performances," *Science* 323, no. 5918 (February 27, 2009): 1226–1229, https://www.science.org/doi/10.1126/science.1169144.

4. I. Song et al., "Effects of nature sounds on the attention and physiological and psychological relaxation," *Urban Forestry and Urban Greening* 86 (August 2023), https://www.sciencedirect.com/science/article/pii/S1618866723001589.

5. C.-H. Hsieh et al., "The effect of water sound level in virtual reality: A study of

restorative benefits in young adults through immersive natural environments," *Journal of Environmental Psychology* 88 (2023): 102012, https://doi.org/10.1016/j.jenvp.2023.102012.

6. H. Shweta and S. Sobhan, "Dynamics of water and ions around DNA: What is so special about them?" *Journal of Biosciences* 43, no. 3 (2018): 499–518, https://pubmed.ncbi.nlm.nih.gov/30002269/.

7. American Meteorological Society, "Lenard Effect," *Glossary of Meteorology*, accessed July 7, 2025, https://glossary.ametsoc.org/wiki/Lenard_effect.

8. K. Fukui et al., "Effect of extract-added water derived from deep-sea water with different hardness on cognitive function, motor ability, and serum indexes of obese mice," *Nutrients* 14, no. 9 (2022): 1794, doi:10.3390/nu14091794.

CHAPTER SIXTEEN: DOPAMINE PUSH-UPS

1. D. Lieberman and M. E. Long, *The Molecule of More* (BenBella Books, 2018), p. 16.

2. T. Haynes, "Dopamine, smartphones, and you: A battle for your time" (May 1, 2018), https://sites.harvard.edu/sitn/2018/05/01/dopamine-smartphones-battle-time/.

3. M. Vasa, conversation with Laura Rubin, May 13, 2024.

4. M. Fuchs, "How to get healthier dopamine highs," *Time* (March 7, 2022), https://time.com/6155109/healthier-dopamine-highs/.

5. J. Waters, "Constant craving: How digital media turned us all into dopamine addicts," *Guardian* (August 22, 2021), https://www.theguardian.com/global/2021/aug/22/how-digital-media-turned-us-all-into-dopamine-addicts-and-what-we-can-do-to-break-the-cycle.

6. S. Krach et al., "The rewarding nature of social interactions," *Frontiers in Behavioral Neuroscience* (May 28, 2010), https://pmc.ncbi.nlm.nih.gov/articles/PMC2889690/.

7. J. Ho, "How to boost dopamine naturally," *Psychology Today* (September 20, 2024), https://www.psychologytoday.com/us/blog/unlock-your-true-motivation/202409/how-to-boost-dopamine-naturally.

8. L. C. Dang et al., "Reduced effects of age on dopamine D2 receptor levels in physically active adults," *NeuroImage* (January 10, 2017), https://pubmed.ncbi.nlm.nih.gov/28089678/.

9. R. D. Andar, "3 activities to beneficially release dopamine," *Psychology Today* (March 23, 2024), https://www.psychologytoday.com/us/blog/understanding-hypnosis/202402/3-activities-to-beneficially-release-dopamine.

CHAPTER SEVENTEEN: TIMES TWO

1. Cleveland Clinic, "Everything you need to know about habit stacking for self-improvement," *Health Essentials* (last modified June 18, 2024), https://health.clevelandclinic.org/habit-stacking.

2. J. Nash, "The history of meditation: Its origins and timeline," *PositivePsychology.com* (last modified May 27, 2019), https://positivepsychology.com/history-of-meditation/.

CHAPTER EIGHTEEN: VICTORY LAP

1. "Why 'crowding out' is the healthiest way to diet," *Integrative Nutrition* (blog) (updated November 6, 2024), https://www.integrativenutrition.com/blog/2016/10/why-crowding-out-is-the-healthiest-way-to-diet.

CHAPTER NINETEEN: WELCOME HOME (TO YOUR BODY)

1. B. van der Kolk, *The Body Keeps the Score: Brain, Mind, and Body in the Healing of Trauma* (Penguin, 2015).

2. "Spleen," Cleveland Clinic (April 29, 2021), https://my.clevelandclinic.org/health/body/21567-spleen.

3. K. Turner, *Radical Hope* (Hay House, 2021), p. 120.

CHAPTER TWENTY: BOREDOM IS UNDERRATED

1. K. Weir, "Never a dull moment," *Monitor on Psychology* 44, no. 7 (July/August 2013), https://www.apa.org/monitor/2013/07-08/dull-moment.

2. S. Mann, *The Science of Boredom: The Upside (and Downside) of Downtime* (Robinson, 2018).

3. Andrea Appleton, "Cultivating creativity," *Think* (Spring/Summer 2014), Case Western Reserve University, https://case.edu/think/spring2014/cultivating-creativity.html.

4. D. Rotman, "We're not prepared for the end of Moore's Law," *MIT Technology Review* (February 24, 2020), https://www.technologyreview.com/2020/02/24/905789/were-not-prepared-for-the-end-of-moores-law/.

5. S. G. Cusick, "Music as torture/Music as weapon," *Trans: Revista Transcultural de Música*, no. 10 (2006), https://www.sibetrans.com/trans/articulo/152/music-as-torture-music-as-weapon.

CHAPTER TWENTY-TWO: THE GRATEFUL HEAD

1. A. J. Smith, "Gratitude: A mental health game changer," *Anxiety & Depression Association of America*, accessed February 27, 2025, https://adaa.org/learn-from-us/from-the-experts/blog-posts/consumer/gratitude-mental-health-game-changer.

2. J. S. Price, "Evolutionary aspects of anxiety disorders," *Dialogues in Clinical Neuroscience* 5, no. 3 (2003): 223–236, https://doi.org/10.31887/DCNS.2003.5.3/jprice.

3. A. Lau-Zhu et al., "Selective association between Tetris game play and visuospatial working memory: A preliminary investigation," *Applied Cognitive Psychology* 31, no. 4 (2017): 438–445, doi:10.1002/acp.3339.

4. M. Shaver, "Tetris and the Game Boy: A Perfect Pairing," *New York Times* (March 31, 2023), https://www.nytimes.com/2023/03/31/movies/tetris-game-boy-nintendo.html.

5. R. A. Emmons, "Gratitude and well-being," Emmons Lab, University of California, Davis, accessed February 27, 2025, https://emmons.faculty.ucdavis.edu/gratitude-and-well-being/.

6. M. R. Chowdhury, "The neuroscience of gratitude and effects on the brain," *Positive Psychology* (April 9, 2019), https://positivepsychology.com/neuroscience-of-gratitude/.

7. S. B. Algoe and R. Zhaoyang, "Positive psychology in context: Effects of expressing

gratitude in ongoing relationships depend on perceptions of enactor responsiveness," *Journal of Positive Psychology* 11, no. 4 (2016): 399–415, https://doi.org/10.1080/17439760.2015.1117131.

8. M. Salamon, "Gratitude enhances health, brings happiness—and may even lengthen lives," Harvard Health Publishing (September 11, 2024), https://www.health.harvard.edu/blog/gratitude-enhances-health-brings-happiness-and-may-even-lengthen-lives-202409113071.

CHAPTER TWENTY-THREE: THE WELLNESS TRAP

1. *Global Wellness Economy Monitor* 2024 (Global Wellness Institute, November 2024), https://globalwellnessinstitute.org/industry-research/2024-global-wellness-economy-monitor/.

2. R. F. Baumeister et al., "Bad is stronger than good," *Review of General Psychology* 5, no. 4 (2001): 323–370, https://psycnet.apa.org/record/2018-70020-001.

3. C. Littlefield, "Do compliments make you cringe? Here's why," *Harvard Business Review* (April 2, 2021), https://hbr.org/2021/04/do-compliments-make-you-cringe-heres-why.

4. D. Chen et al., "Negative association between resilience and event-related potentials evoked by negative emotion," *Scientific Reports* 8, no. 1 (May 2018), doi: 10.1038/s41598-018-25555-w.

CHAPTER TWENTY-FOUR: GROUP SWIM

1. G. Shteynberg et al., "Theory of collective mind," *Trends in Cognitive Sciences* 27, no. 11 (2023): 1019–1031, https://doi.org/10.1016/j.tics.2023.06.009.

2. M. O. Brigano, "Parallel play," in S. Goldstein et al., eds., *Encyclopedia of Child Behavior and Development* (Springer, 2011), https://doi.org/10.1007/978-0-387-79061-9_2073.

3. B. C. Feeney, "The dependency paradox in close relationships: Accepting dependence promotes independence," *Journal of Personality and Social Psychology* 92, no. 2 (2007): 268–285, doi:10.1037/0022-3514.92.2.268.

CHAPTER TWENTY-FIVE: COUPLED UP

1. L. R. Lapping-Carr, "The science of love: What's happening in your body," *Northwestern Medicine* (February 2024), https://www.nm.org/healthbeat/healthy-tips/emotional-health/the-science-of-love.

2. B. Condor, "A chemistry lesson for lovers," *Chicago Tribune* (February 9, 2000), https://www.chicagotribune.com/2000/02/09/a-chemistry-lesson-for-lovers/.

3. B. B. Jardine et al., "Emotional intelligence and romantic relationship satisfaction: A systematic review and meta-analysis," *Personality and Individual Differences* 196 (2022): 111713, https://doi.org/10.1016/j.paid.2022.111713.

4. R. B. Slatcher and J. W. Pennebaker, "How do I love thee? Let me count the words: The social effects of expressive writing," *Psychological Science* 17, no. 8 (2006): 660–664, https://doi.org/10.1111/j.1467-9280.2006.01762.x.

5. D. Griffin et al., "The self-fulfilling nature of positive illusions in romantic

relationships: Love is not blind but prescient," *Journal of Personality and Social Psychology* 71, no. 6 (1996): 1155–1180, https://www.researchgate.net/publication/14229345_The_Self-Fulfilling_Nature_of_Positive_Illusions_in_Romantic_Relationships_Love_Is_Not_Blind_but_Prescient.

CHAPTER TWENTY-SIX: BYE-BYE, BLOCKS

1. A. Mangen et al., "Handwriting versus keyboard writing: Effect on word recall," *Journal of Writing Research* 7 (2015): 227–247, doi:10.17239/jowr-2015.07.02.1.

2. M. Oppezzo and D. L. Schwartz: "Give your ideas some legs: The positive effect of walking on creative thinking," *Journal of Experimental Psychology, Learning, Memory, and Cognition* 40, no. 4 (2014): 1142–1152, doi:10.1037/a0036577.

3. A. Basu et al., "Attention restoration theory: Exploring the role of soft fascination and mental bandwidth," *Environment and Behavior* 51, no. 9–10 (2019): 1055–1081, https://doi.org/10.1177/0013916518774400.

4. A. Basu, J. Duvall, and R. Kaplan, "Attention restoration."

5. "Restoring your exhausted and tired brain through soft fascinations," *The Willows* (blog), accessed January 28, 2025, https://www.thewillows.org/wisdom-of-the-willows/~board/blog-articles/post/restoring-your-exhausted-and-tired-brain-through-soft-fascinations.

6. T. P. Pham and T. Sanocki, "Human attention restoration, flow, and creativity: A conceptual integration," *Journal of Imaging* 10, no. 4 (2024): 83, doi:10.3390/jimaging10040083.

CHAPTER TWENTY-SEVEN: PERMISSION SLIPS

1. Queensland Brain Institute, "What is neurogenesis?" University of Queensland, accessed January 28, 2025, https://qbi.uq.edu.au/brain-basics/brain-physiology/what-neurogenesis#:~:text=Neurogenesis%20is%20the%20process%20by,birth%20and%20throughout%20our%20lifespan.

2. T. J. Shors et al., "Use it or lose it: How neurogenesis keeps the brain fit for learning," *Behavioural Brain Research* 227, no. 2 (2012): 450–458, doi: 10.1016/j.bbr.2011.04.023.

3. P. Eriksson et al., "Neurogenesis in the adult human hippocampus," *Nature Medicine* 4 (1998): 1313–1317, https://doi.org/10.1038/3305.

4. M. Solan, "The book of neurogenesis," Harvard Health Publishing (August 1, 2021), https://www.health.harvard.edu/mind-and-mood/the-book-of-neurogenesis.

5. B. Winner and Jürgen Winkler, "Adult neurogenesis in neurodegenerative diseases," *Cold Spring Harbor Perspectives in Biology* 7, no. 4 (2015): a021287, doi:10.1101/cshperspect.a021287.

6. C. Raypole, "6 ways to rewire your brain," *Healthline* (November 1, 2024), https://www.healthline.com/health/rewiring-your-brain#exercise.

7. A. Felman, "5 neuroplasticity exercises to try," *Medical News Today* (August 18, 2023), https://www.medicalnewstoday.com/articles/neuroplasticity-exercises.

8. D. M. Durant, *Reading in a Digital Age* (University of Michigan Press, 2019), accessed January 28, 2025, http://dx.doi.org/10.3998/mpub.9944117.

9. D. I. Tamir et al., "Reading fiction and reading minds: The role of simulation in the default network," *Social Cognitive and Affective Neuroscience* 11, no. 2 (2015): 215–224, doi:10.1093/scan/nsv114.

10. L. Ping et al., "Neuroplasticity as a function of second language learning: Anatomical changes in the human brain," *Cortex* 49, no. 2 (2013): 338–340, https://doi.org/10.1016/j.cortex.2012.10.007.

11. R. Fang et al., "Music therapy is a potential intervention for cognition of Alzheimer's disease: A mini-review," *Translational Neurodegeneration* 6, no. 2 (2017), https://doi.org/10.1186/s40035-017-0073-9.

12. D. W. Zaidel, "Art and brain: Insights from neuropsychology, biology, and evolution," *Journal of Anatomy* 216, no. 2 (2010): 177–183, doi:10.1111/j.1469-7580.2009.01099.x.

13. Queensland Brain Institute, "Adult neurogenesis," University of Queensland, accessed January 28, 2025, https://qbi.uq.edu.au/brain-basics/brain-physiology/adult-neurogenesis.

14. M. Gorgoni et al., "Is sleep essential for neural plasticity in humans, and how does it affect motor and cognitive recovery?" *Neural Plasticity* 2013, no. 4 (2013): 103949, doi:10.1155/2013/103949.

15. L. Teixeira-Machado et al., "Dance for neuroplasticity: A descriptive systematic review," *Neuroscience and Biobehavioral Reviews* 96, no. 10 (2019): 232–240, doi:10.1016/j.neubiorev.2018.12.010.

16. B. R. Kouba and A. L. S. Rodrigues, "Neuroplasticity-related effects of vitamin D relevant to its neuroprotective effects: A narrative review," *Pharmacology Biochemistry and Behavior* 245 (2024): 173899, https://doi.org/10.1016/j.pbb.2024.173899.

17. Z-P. Xu et al., "Magnesium protects cognitive functions and synaptic plasticity in streptozotocin-induced sporadic Alzheimer's model," *PLOS One* 9, no. 9 (2014): e108645, doi:10.1371/journal.pone.0108645.

18. J. L. Ong et al., "A daytime nap restores hippocampal function and improves declarative learning," *Sleep* 43, no. 9 (2020): zsaa058; doi:10.1093/sleep/zsaa058.

19. B. A. Philip and S. H. Frey, "Increased functional connectivity between cortical hand areas and praxis network associated with training-related improvements in non-dominant hand precision drawing," *Neuropsychologia* 87 (2016): 157–168, doi:10.1016/j.neuropsychologia.2016.05.016.

CHAPTER TWENTY-EIGHT: SLOW YOUR ROLL

1. A. Tank, "The psychological benefits of writing by hand," *Fast Company* (November 23, 2020), accessed February 27, 2025, https://www.fastcompany.com/90578555/the-psychological-benefits-of-writing-by-hand.

2. N. Olson, "Three ways that writing with a pen positively affects your brain," *Forbes* (May 15, 2016), accessed February 27, 2025, https://www.forbes.com/sites/nancyolson/2016/05/15/three-ways-that-writing-with-a-pen-positively-affects-your-brain/.

3. "Rorschach Test," *Psychology Today*, accessed February 27, 2025, https://www.psychologytoday.com/us/basics/rorschach-test.

4. B. Barratt, "Sensuality, sexuality, and the eroticism of slowness," in *Culture of the Slow*, ed. by Nick Osbaldiston (Palgrave Macmillan, 2013), doi:10.1057/9781137319449_8.

5. K. Hawton et al., "Slow down: Behavioural and physiological effects of reducing eating rate," *Nutrients* 11, no. 1 (December 2018): 50, doi:10.3390/nu11010050.

6. N. Matthews et al., "Media-multitasking and cognitive control across the lifespan," *Scientific Reports* 12, article 4349 (2022), https://doi.org/10.1038/s41598-022-07777-1.

CHAPTER TWENTY-NINE: DON'T QUIT BEFORE THE MIRACLE

1. Olivia Harrison, interview by Martin Scorsese, in George Harrison, *Living in the Material World*, directed by Martin Scorsese (Warner Bros. Pictures, 2011), at 1:19:13.

CHAPTER THIRTY: SOLID SELF-WORTH

1. C. Geng, "Tall poppy syndrome: What to know," *Medical News Today* (last modified June 24, 2024), https://www.medicalnewstoday.com/articles/tall-poppy-syndrome.

2. S. B. Kaufman, "Narcissism and self-esteem are very different," *Scientific American* (October 29, 2017), https://www.scientificamerican.com/blog/beautiful-minds/narcissism-and-self-esteem-are-very-different/.

CHAPTER THIRTY-TWO: THE BREAKUP HANDBOOK

1. K. G. Seshadri, "The neuroendocrinology of love," *Indian Journal of Endocrinology and Metabolism* 20, no. 4 (2016): 558–563, https://doi.org/10.4103/2230-8210.183479.

2. S. Edwards, "Love on the brain," *Harvard Medical School* (Spring 2015), accessed February 27, 2025, https://hms.harvard.edu/news-events/publications-archive/brain/love-brain.

3. B. Condor, "A chemistry lesson for lovers," *Chicago Tribune* (February 9, 2000), https://www.chicagotribune.com/2000/02/09/a-chemistry-lesson-for-lovers/.

4. S. Edwards, "Love on the brain."

5. Z. Zou et al., "Romantic love vs. drug addiction may inspire a new treatment for addiction," *Frontiers in Psychology* 7 (2016): 1436, https://doi.org/10.3389/fpsyg.2016.01436.

6. Cleveland Clinic, "Why giving is good for your health," Health Essentials (December 7, 2022), https://health.clevelandclinic.org/why-giving-is-good-for-your-health.

CHAPTER THIRTY-THREE: HEAVY WEATHER

1. R. E. Lucas and N. M. Lawless, "Does life seem better on a sunny day? Examining the association between daily weather conditions and life satisfaction judgments," *Journal*

of Personality and Social Psychology 104, no. 5 (2013): 872–884, doi:10.1037/a0032124.

2. Z. Wyatt, "The dark side of #PositiveVibes: Understanding toxic positivity in modern culture," *Psychiatry and Behavioral Health* 3, no. 1 (2024): 1–6, https://www.researchgate.net/publication/383871051_The_Dark_Side_of_PositiveVibes_Understanding_Toxic_Positivity_in_Modern_Culture.

3. A. Rolston and E. Lloyd-Richardson, "What is emotion regulation?" Cornell Research Program on Self-Injury and Recovery, accessed March 10, 2025, https://selfinjury.bctr.cornell.edu/perch/resources/what-is-emotion-regulationsinfo-brief.pdf.

4. A. S. Cowen and D. Keltner, "Self-report captures 27 distinct categories of emotion bridged by continuous gradients," *Proceedings of the National Academy of Sciences* 114, no. 38 (2017): E7900–E7909, https://doi.org/10.1073/pnas.1702247114.

CHAPTER THIRTY-FOUR: GOOD GRIEF

1. P. Tyrrell et al., "Kubler-Ross stages of dying and subsequent models of grief," National Library of Medicine (updated February 26, 2023), https://www.ncbi.nlm.nih.gov/books/NBK507885/.

2. E. Kübler-Ross and D. Kessler, *On Grief and Grieving: Finding the Meaning of Grief Through the Five Stages of Loss* (Simon and Schuster, 2014), https://www.simonandschuster.com/books/On-Grief-and-Grieving/Elisabeth-Kubler-Ross/9781476775555.

3. E. Kübler-Ross and D. Kessler, *On Grief and Grieving.*

4. E. Griswold, "How 'Silent Spring' ignited the environmental movement," *New York Times Magazine* (September 21, 2012), https://www.nytimes.com/2012/09/23/magazine/how-silent-spring-ignited-the-environmental-movement.html.

5. G. Hendrick, "The influence of Thoreau's 'Civil Disobedience' on Gandhi's Satyagraha," *New England Quarterly* 29, no. 4 (1956): 462–471, https://doi.org/10.2307/362139.

6. B. Powell, "Henry David Thoreau, Martin Luther King Jr., and the American tradition of protest," *OAH Magazine of History* 9, no. 2 (Winter 1995): 26–29, https://doi.org/10.1093/maghis/9.2.26.

7. B. van der Kolk, *The Body Keeps the Score: Brain, Mind, and Body in the Healing of Trauma* (Penguin, 2015).

CHAPTER THIRTY-FIVE: IN PRAISE OF THE LONG GAME

1. "W. S. Merwin," *Poetry Foundation*, accessed March 10, 2025, https://www.poetryfoundation.org/poets/w-s-merwin.

2. "How poet W. S. Merwin found paradise by planting palm trees," PBS News Hour (February 20, 2015), https://www.pbs.org/newshour/show/poet-w-s-merwin-found-paradise-planting-palm-trees.

ABOUT THE AUTHOR

LAURA L. RUBIN, journaling expert, creative coach, and founder of mindful writing company AllSwell Creative, has changed the cultural conversation about what it means to journal. Sought after as a speaker and facilitator (and celebrated in media including *The New York Times*, *The Washington Post*, *Vogue*, and *Forbes*), Rubin has, over the past decade, hosted hundreds of "breakthrough writing" workshops for tens of thousands of participants about the wide-ranging, scientifically proven benefits of putting pen to paper. Tapping her professional experience as corporate executive, journalist and entrepreneur, Rubin has brought journaling to surprising places and audiences, from professional athletes to venture capital firms. To broaden AllSwell's reach, Rubin established EndsWell, a nonprofit program pairing trained journaling workshop facilitators with communities in need. She lives in Sag Harbor, New York. Visit AllSwellCreative.com for more information.